D0197817

JESUS, AUTHOR OF OUR FAITH

A·W·TOZER

Jesus, Author of Our Faith

COMPILED AND EDITED BY
GERALD B. SMITH

CHRISTIAN PUBLICATIONS
Camp Hill, Pennsylvania

Christian Publications
3825 Hartzdale Drive, Camp Hill, PA 17011

The mark of ✝ vibrant faith

ISBN: 0-87509-406-6
LOC Catalog Card Number: 88-70129
© 1988 by Christian Publications

Cover photo: "The Commissioning of The Twelve," Zion Lutheran Church, Harrisburg, PA. Photo by Mike Saunier.

CONTENTS

FOREWORD

TOZER ONCE WARNED Christian believers not to read the Bible as they would another piece of literature or a textbook. "I have always felt that when we read and study the Word of God, we should have great expectations," he explained. "We should ask the Holy Spirit to reveal the person, the glory and the eternal ministry of our Lord Jesus Christ."

This book is centered on Jesus. It is based on sermons Tozer preached from the final chapters of the Letter to the Hebrews. The author's intention, from chapter to chapter, is to underscore the necessity of an active, abiding faith in Jesus Christ. Only in that way can we please God.

More than in most of his books, Tozer reaches into his personal experience as he applies the rich truths of key texts. For that reason, it is fitting that the publisher will release this volume in May 1988 – exactly 25 years after Tozer's death on May 13, 1963.

For those who try to collect Tozer titles as they become available, it should be pointed out that *Jesus, Author of Our Faith* is a companion volume to *Jesus, Our Man in Glory*, which is based on the earlier chapters of Hebrews. Together, the two books examine most of the important emphases in that significant Letter. They do so in Tozer's inimitable style and with his incisive expression.

Gerald B. Smith

1

Jesus, Author of Our Faith

DO YOU REALIZE THAT YOUR FAITH is a gift from God? You should look upon your faith as a miracle. It is the ability God gives lost men and women to trust and obey our Savior and Lord. It is the ability God gives regenerated men and women to continue to trust and obey.

And Jesus is the author of our faith.

Are you satisfied, contented with your faith? Is it the kind of faith that is pleasing to God? Does it rest solidly upon the very nature and character of God? I raise these questions with the hope of finding some ripple of concern among God's people about this simple, straightforward statement in the letter to the Hebrews: "Without faith, it is impossible to please God."

In all of my ministry I have found comparatively few eager to consider what the Bible teaches concerning genuine faith in God. It is difficult, also, to find spiritual concern among Christians for trusting God and living to please the One who created us and who redeemed us back to Himself.

The 11th chapter of Hebrews is often called "The Faith Chapter." Its opening message is familiar:

> Now faith is being sure of what we hope for and certain of what we do not see. . . . By faith we understand that the universe was formed at

God's command, so that what is seen was not made out of what was visible. . . . And without faith it is impossible to please God, because anyone who comes to him must believe that he exists and that he rewards those who earnestly seek him. (Hebrews 11:1–6)

"The Faith Chapter." I doubt that most people recognize the full meaning of that term, "the faith chapter." I would like to amend the title by calling Hebrews 11 the "Faith-in-God Chapter." Or, even better, the "Faith-in-the-Character-of-God Chapter."

The word *faith* can mean a thousand different things to as many people. It is especially so if in their thinking there is no basic reference to God, no consideration of His eternal will and no understanding of the lostness of mankind. I have discovered that professing Christians can read about the great exploits of faith in the past—and then immediately ask the age-old question, "But what is faith?"

No actual definition

Although the writer to the Hebrews declares that faith is being sure of what we hope for and being certain of what we do not see, he is not thereby actually providing us with a definition. Definitions have to do with human reason, human intellect, human philosophy. I think God had His own reasons for withholding a specific definition of faith from the pages of our Bibles.

God's record and appeal are spiritual messages, directed to the spirits of needy men and women. If our Christian testimony is to be vital and effective, we must understand that the Bible was not given to serve as a handbook of ethical considerations. Rather, it is plainly a book of morals. Therefore, when we take God at His word in committing ourselves to Jesus Christ, we discover that faith and morals are two sides of the same coin!

I repeat: The Bible is not a book of reason about things that are good and things that are bad. Rather, it is an authoritative book clearly demonstrating for us what *is* good and what *is* bad! On that basis, then, what does the Bible tell us about genuine faith?

Without dealing in pinpoint definitions, we know that faith as demonstrated in the Word of God is complete confidence and trust in God and in His plan of salvation through Christ.

Let us agree further that faith is a gift of God to every penitent, trusting person. Beyond that, faith is a miracle, for God gives lost men and women the blessed ability to trust and serve Jesus Christ as Savior and Lord.

The Bible assures us that faith in God is the plain gateway to forgiveness, to cleansing, to regeneration, to restoration. The Bible declares that where there is no faith there are no answers to fervent prayers. The Bible makes clear that every spiritual benefit flowing from the atonement of Christ is given to faith and is received by faith. All of this is common evangelical doctrine and is accepted wherever the cross of Christ is rightly understood.

Beware of faith in "faith"

I have often warned men in the ministry of their

great responsibility when they begin to preach and counsel about faith. It is quite possible to lead people into the mistake of placing their faith in "faith" itself.

I do not think any of us believes that as Christians we can or should ever be satisfied by emphasizing our faith in "faith." To do so would result in our bragging about the greatness of our faith and our trading mutual testimonies about the results of *our* faith.

I remember an old story, used more than once as sermon illustration. It concerned an anonymous Christian believer who testified of great faith and willing obedience with this rather amazing promise: "If the Lord ever asks me to jump right through that brick wall, I am ready to jump!"

My point is that we should not be busy magnifying our own great faith. Rather, we should be busy demonstrating the fragrance of God's love and grace in our daily walk. It is not proper to magnify faith if in doing so we forget that our confidence as believers is not in the power of faith but in the person and work of our Savior, Jesus Christ.

I have heard ministers say that if the people in their congregations would memorize more Bible promises, they would immediately have more faith. Yes and no.

Study the Scriptures and you will find that we are not going to have more faith by counting the promises of God. Faith does not rest upon promises. Faith rests upon character. Faith must rest in confidence upon the One who makes the promises.

Faith says, "God is God! He is a holy God who

cannot lie. He is the God who is infinitely honest –
He has never cheated anyone. He is the God who is
faithful and true!"

Yes, we must be concerned with the person and
character of God and not just with His promises.
Through promises we learn what God has willed to
us, we learn what we may claim as our heritage, we
learn how we should pray. But faith itself must rest
upon the character of our God.

When I think of the angels in heaven who veil
their faces before the holy God who is totally truth-
ful, I wonder why every preacher does not begin
preaching about God – who He is, His attributes,
His perfection, His being and why we love Him
and why we should trust Him!

We must know God Himself

It is not enough just to know things about God. It
is important that we declare to people all round us
that they must come to know God Himself.

Our faith in God is more than the provision of an
eternal life insurance policy. Some Christians in
their testimonies seem to view God as a lifeboat
always coming to their rescue. Or perhaps they
portray Him as a kind of ladder enabling them to
get out of a burning building.

We dare not miss the point here. Our God takes
pleasure in His believing children coming to Him
with genuine faith, knowing that He is the rewarder of all who diligently seek Him. This kind of
earnest, genuine faith – the faith of the Scriptures –
is taught and fully demonstrated in this book of
Hebrews.

The lesson that comes to us through the many dramatic illustrations of faith in Hebrews 11 brings us back to my earlier statement: Faith in God is to be demonstrated, not defined. Just as God's church demonstrates Christian love, this demonstration of godly, humble faith is God's ideal for His church.

It is not enough for preachers in their pulpits to try to define love. The love that God has promised must be demonstrated in the lives of the believers in the pews. It must be practiced as well by the man who occupies the pulpit.

We should put the matter of faith in that same category. God wants His people, including the ministers, to demonstrate all of the outworking of faith in their daily lives and practices.

In His Word, God tells us again and again that as believing children we are to live by faith and we are to walk by faith. This reference is to God's believing, trusting people and to the kind of faith that is saving faith. There are many other brands of faith being displayed in our world today. Saving faith — biblical faith — is on the highest level, for it is the life of trust and obedience that our Lord requires of us.

The Bible says faith is necessary to please God. It is plain, then, that there are unbelievers — men and women without faith who refuse to take God into consideration. It is my position that unbelief is not merely a different attitude of the human mind. Unbelief is always sinful because it presupposes an immoral condition of the heart.

The unbeliever says in effect to the Christian believer: "My gift of human reason tells me that you are unreasonable in the matters of your faith."

Christians have an answer

Christian believers have an answer born from their scriptural perspective. They are not afraid to declare that at the door of the kingdom of God man's reason is dethroned. For those who are living a life of faith and have found fellowship with God, human reason is no longer king. Instead, reason becomes a servant.

The apostle Paul warned the Corinthian Christians long ago that God had made foolish the wisdom of the world:

> But God chose the foolish things of the world to shame the wise . . . so that no one may boast before him. . . . Therefore, as it is written: "Let him who boasts boast in the Lord." (1 Corinthians 1:27–31)

Human reason has always been in rivalry with God. Our human race took a great fall on the day Satan persuaded Adam and Eve to disobey their Creator God. He told them it was *reasonable* that they should have the same knowledge that God Himself has. Our first parents bowed to reason, taking the bait like hungry fish.

We are only too well aware of the results of their failure—their disobedience. Instead of becoming as gods in knowledge, they and their posterity fell to such a low level that they lost their capacity to know anything that really matters!

I am asked sometimes for my opinion on certain matters. Perhaps you would like to ask my opinion concerning the faculty of human reason, and I am ready to answer even before you ask! I believe that most people are more proud of their ability to reason than of any other faculty. They do not even suspect that nothing else they possess is as small as their power to reason.

Once those persons enter the kingdom of God by faith, reason becomes a useful servant—no longer ruling them as a false god. On the other hand, those who continue to live without Christ and without God will unknowingly live out their lives in a very real kind of sub-faith, strange as that may seem.

The rationalists exercise faith

I confess that it is very intriguing to me to consider the habits of the so-called liberal thinkers. They reject the validity of any kind of faith, declaring that they choose to reject religion because it requires faith. Yet they do not discern that they are going through many of the motions of faith every day.

They get up every morning fully expecting that the sun will be in its accustomed course when they rise. They fully expect that the morning newspaper will be delivered as promised. Although they cannot entirely explain it, they have no doubt that breakfast will satisfy their appetites—at least temporarily!

They step out on the sidewalk with full faith that it will not collapse under their weight. They do not call the office where they work to inquire if they still have a job. Something very much like faith tells them their job is secure and waiting.

Nearly every move they make is by a certain kind of faith and trust. Their boast is that they lean only on reason, but from dawn until bedtime their lives fit into a pattern of faith and trust, whether they admit it or not! Yet they will argue and debate at every possible opportunity that faith is unreal and cannot be accepted because it is not predicated on human reasoning.

We who are believing Christians refuse to agree with the unbelievers' premise that we are taking an unreasonable position. We simply accept our new realm of life and faith where reason becomes a servant. We find a blessed fulfillment in a life of trust.

We discover in this relationship with God that faith actually becomes an organ of knowledge. That is why it is completely ridiculous for religious prattlers to insist that they can equate faith and reason.

According to both Matthew and Luke, Jesus prayed, saying: "I praise you, Father, Lord of heaven and earth, because you have hidden these things from the wise and learned, and revealed them to little children." Yes, we do find that faith becomes an organ of knowledge.

In Hebrews we read, "By faith we understand that the universe was formed at God's command, so that what is seen was not made out of what was visible" (11:3).

The proud thinkers tell us they believe in the eternity of matter. They are convinced in their own minds that there was never a time when things were not. To them, matter is eternal. For them, there is no invisible, eternal world back of the visible, temporal world we see and know.

The Bible tells us otherwise

But we lean on the inspired Word from the Holy Spirit of God, who gives us this truth: The visible came out of the invisible. It was God who framed the worlds. The things that are seen came from the Unseen. Thus we learn that matter came out of spirit, and before all things was God Himself!

It is by faith that we can understand these things. And that is another way of saying, "By faith we know!" We know, too, that there is much imagination in the world. For that reason we contend that our faith is not a substitute for reality. Faith in God apprehends reality and spiritual things.

True faith is not a function of imagination. I disagree with the modern theories that peace and happiness depend upon our ability to "project" ourselves out of subconscious minds. The proponents of that philosophy would have us believe that the subconscious mind sits around waiting for the conscious mind to talk to it. Then, if the conscious mind is willing to say to the subconscious, "You are going to feel good today!" you will really feel good all day.

That is human imagination. Faith in God is a function of knowledge, not of human imagination. We do not by faith project out of ourselves an imaginary hope of heaven beyond this life. Jesus Christ has promised that our place is being prepared; it is a promise of our Heavenly Father.

I tell you frankly that I would not want to consider any kind of a heaven that was projected out of my subconscious mind. I am looking forward to something far more substantial than a projection of my own mind or imagination!

What the Bible says

Now, if we really have a desire for our faith in God to increase and grow, do we have any New Testament direction or encouragement? Yes! We can take a lesson from the conversation about faith between Jesus and His disciples:

> The apostles said to the Lord, "Increase our faith!"
>
> He replied, "If you have faith as small as a mustard seed, you can say to this mulberry tree, 'Be uprooted and planted in the sea,' and it will obey you." (Luke 17:5–6)

The apostles apparently recognized their own need and addressed a direct prayer to the Author of faith—their Lord and Master: "Increase our faith!" Did Jesus reprove them for their earnest request, for their desire to mature in the realm of faith? No. Jesus did not reprove nor did He rebuke.

Instead, He taught them and He encouraged them. Surely it should strike us with conviction that our Lord was saying that even to the smallest measure of sincere faith the mightiest works for God are possible.

I ask: Do you believe as earnestly as you should that faith can bring the conversion of the human soul to God? Do you believe as deeply as you should that faith can unite you forever to Jesus Christ, your risen Lord and now your great High Priest in the heavens?

Do you believe as you should that earnest and sincere faith in the living God can remove mountains of difficulty out of your way, can cast your burden of guilt into the deepest sea? The Author of our faith stands ready to make it so.

A concluding illustration

Let me conclude with a contemporary illustration of faith easily understood because it could happen in any family household.

A father and his nine-year-old son have a close and trusting relationship. The father reminds his boy that in a month he will be observing his 10th birthday.

"Son," he begins, "I know that you want a bicycle. I am going to order a brand new red and white bicycle, and it will be here in time for you to begin riding it on the morning of your birthday. It will be your very own bicycle—you will be the owner!"

Is that excited boy going to wait a month before he tells his friends that he is the owner of a shining new bicycle? Oh, no! He runs out immediately to give the great news to his friends. He is full of faith. He is full of expectancy. He already knows within himself the pride of ownership. His faith has given substance to his boyish hope. His faith has given a reality to the bicycle he has not yet seen!

He is not reporting to his friends an imaginary projection of his mind. He has his father's word. He is able to speak with assurance: "Believe it or not, I own one of the most beautiful bicycles in the whole world!"

That boy knows he can trust the character of his father. His faith is not in the factory that makes the bicycle. It rests in the character and the ability of his father to keep the promise he has made.

But, of course, there is one little friend in the neighborhood who remains cynical and unbelieving.

"Don't give me that dreamy line about having a bicycle," the friend insists with some belligerence. "Who is going to believe your story? I don't see any shiny new bicycle in your front yard."

For an answer, the boy with the faith, the boy who already knows the delight of anticipation, simply smiles a knowing smile. "Just give me till my birthday, and when you see me riding my bike past your house, you will wish my father was your father, too!"

We thank our Heavenly Father that our sincere faith in Him becomes for us a function of knowledge. It becomes substance and evidence!

Jesus is the Author and the Perfecter of our faith. With the apostle Paul we stand in faith and in knowledge: "I am not ashamed, because I know whom I have believed, and am convinced that he is able to guard what I have entrusted to him for that day" (2 Timothy 1:12).

Enoch: Faith Takes Us to the Rapture

T HERE IS A GREAT COMPANY of believers within the Christian church in our day willing to take God at His word when He says our world is headed for judgment. On the other hand, there are many who scoff at the idea of judgment and contend that everything around us will continue as it is forever and ever.

Some segments within the Christian church believe that God surely is a holy God and that it is possible for men and women of faith to live in a way pleasing to Him. Others presume God expects men and women to find happiness in their own devices. Thus they rule out the validity of the many scriptural warnings as well as the Bible's appeals for godly living.

These observations bring to mind the faith of one man—Enoch—who lived near the beginning of our race. We can only wonder how he would have measured Christianity as we know it in the 20th century!

One of the greatest Bible commentaries on godly faith is the single sentence in Genesis telling us that "Enoch walked with God; then he was no more, because God took him away" (5:24). The New Testament assessment of Enoch's faith is also brief—a single paragraph in the Letter to the Hebrews:

> By faith Enoch was taken from this life, so that he did not experience death; he could not be found, because God had taken him away. For before he was taken, he was commended as one who pleased God. (Hebrews 11:5)

God has given us a faithful and trustworthy record. Any person who refuses to believe the overriding wisdom and illumination of God's Holy Spirit will never have or hold a clear and proper estimate of the human race. In Enoch God has given us an example of faith and a model of daily fellowship with God.

God tells us about His presence

Anyone making even a quick review of Genesis will discover that God has told us more about His presence in creation and in history than about the details of human civilization. In the beginning God created the heavens and the earth. We believe that! That is our starting place. We believe that eternity dwells in the person of God and that the material universe came into being through God's creation.

The first man and woman in the human race were created. They failed in their initial encounter with Satan, our arch enemy. Following that, the Genesis record becomes a narrative of human failure against the abiding backdrop of God's faithfulness.

We are told of Cain and Abel, two sons of Adam and Eve, and of Cain's refusal to honor God's plan for the redemption and acceptance of lost humanity. On the very threshold of human culture and civilization, Cain murdered his brother, Abel. Later, as Cain's wife was giving birth to his first son—an earlier Enoch than the one referred to in Hebrews 11—"Cain was then building a city, and he named it after his son Enoch" (Genesis 4:17).

The civilization founded by Cain was as evil as he. It would ultimately terminate in the judgment of the Flood. But in giving us the brief record of Cain's oldest son, the Spirit of God, as Author of the Bible, binds in one bundle of life all the yesterdays of the race and reveals the organic oneness of all humans.

The information in Genesis is a revelation to our hearts. Through it we understand that all people born of Adam are of one blood. This means that we are bound up in a natural brotherhood throughout the earth. But that does not portray the full and final story.

God Himself, through the Holy Spirit, points out a universal human problem: the natural brotherhood of human beings is a sinful brotherhood. It is the brotherhood of all who are spiritually lost.

But the Bible has good news from the Holy Spirit concerning the human race. That good news is the revelation of a new brotherhood, the brotherhood of the redeemed. We know it in our time as the believing church of our Lord Jesus Christ in all nations.

It is plain that the natural brotherhood that dates back to Adam does not have a saving, redeeming bond. The record is clear for those who will pursue it. God in His love and concern prolonged the race after the Flood. Then in His own time, He called out of the race a chosen people, Israel, in order to ensure the coming of the Messiah-Savior with His gracious offer of salvation and renewal.

The new brotherhood among men is based on regeneration and restoration. Take away the coming of Jesus into the world, take away His redeeming death and His victorious resurrection, and there remains no basis for wholeness and oneness in the race. It is impossible to hold a proper view of mankind's brotherhood without recognizing all that God has done to assure that the eternal brotherhood is the fellowship of redeemed men and women comprising Jesus' church, His Body on earth.

Back to Enoch

But now we have met godly Enoch, seventh generation from Adam through Adam's third son, Seth. We are impressed that he could resist the devil and find fellowship with his Creator-God, even in a worldly society headed for destruction. Enoch recognized the failure of men and women trying to live their lives apart from God and His will. By faith he walked with God on this earth at a time when sin and corruption were wildly rampant all around him.

Enoch's daily walk was a walk of faith, a walk of fellowship with God. What the Scriptures are trying to say to us is this: If Enoch could live and walk with God by faith in the midst of his sinful generation, we likewise should be able to follow his example because the human race is the same and God is the same!

Space does not permit us to cover all the spiritual lessons we might learn from the life of godly Enoch. But I do want to make an important emphasis here for every Christian believer: Enoch reminds us that the quality and boldness of our faith will be the measure of our preparation for the return of Jesus Christ to this earth.

We Christian believers, walking by faith nearly 20 centuries after Christ's sojourn on earth, hold firmly to the New Testament promise that our risen Lord will return to earth again. Our ever-living High Priest in the heavens intends to return for His church—the brotherhood of the redeemed. We are neither ashamed nor afraid to confess our anticipation of Christ's return.

Jesus promised His disciples He would return:

> So, if anyone tells you, "There he is, out in the desert," do not go out; or, "Here he is, in the inner rooms," do not believe it. For as the lightning comes from the east and flashes to the west, so will be the coming of the Son of Man. (Matthew 24:26–27)

Jesus' two appearings are contrasted in this Letter to the Hebrews. First, the writer states the purpose of Jesus' first coming:

> Now he has appeared once for all at the end of the ages to do away with sin by the sacrifice of himself. (Hebrews 9:27)

Then, the writer promises that Christ Jesus will return to bring ultimate salvation to the redeemed:

> So Christ was sacrificed once to take away the

sins of many people; and he will appear a second time, not to bear sin, but to bring salvation to those who are waiting for him. (Hebrews 9:28)

Enoch is a type

I have taken time to point up the Bible promise of Jesus' return for a reason. It is my strong conviction that Enoch's experience of translation into the presence of God is a type,, or preview, of the coming rapture of the church, the bride of Christ, described in the Scriptures.

I can assure you that I have never been a preacher of obscure or curious texts. My calling is to preach the entire Word of God and all of its basic doctrines as revealed by the Holy Spirit of God. I confess that I have been shy about leaning too hard on Bible types or "pictures" in the Word.

I think some teachers have overemphasized the importance of such analogies. Some teachers have mistakenly tried to build doctrines on the types they discerned. It is my advice that we continue to faithfully preach the plain Word of God. We can trust the Holy Spirit to guide us.

In this instance, however, the faith and deportment of the man Enoch do compose a vivid picture—a powerful object lesson—to encourage every Christian believer in his or her faith. Enoch speaks to us of our own troubled times—and that is the purpose of the Word of God. It should be our concern that we hear—and that we obey!

There is only one conclusion to be drawn here. Enoch was translated into the presence of God because of his faith, and thus he escaped death. It is very evident that there was no funeral for Enoch. Those who knew him best surely had to answer many questions. "Where is Enoch?" "What happened to Enoch?" "Why don't we see Enoch around anymore?"

Perhaps members of his own family did not fully understand his walk with God, but they could answer with the facts: "He is gone! God has called him home. God has taken him." I wonder if his contemporaries ever made the obvious comparison: "Enoch always advised us to walk with God—to put our trust in God. We thought he was a fanatic. Now he is gone, he is at home with God, and we are still here in a troubled world!"

Our promised rapture is disparaged

In our own generation, many around us consider our hope in the promise of Christ's return an extreme belief. As the current chapter of church history is being written throughout the world, the teaching of the return of Jesus Christ for His church is not popular.

There probably is no way that we can arrive at the number of believers throughout the breadth and scope of Christianity who consider the prophetic Scriptures seriously. We do know that those who believe and proclaim that Jesus is coming again are in the minority.

Personally, I do not worry or fret about being in the minority where the will of God is concerned. I am firmly persuaded that our Lord Jesus Christ is coming again for His believing people. Throughout my years of ministry, I have held to this teaching found in the Bible. I have had no reason to change my mind concerning it.

This much we know and can say: The general outlines of prophetic events as foretold in the Scriptures are accepted by conservative, evangelical Christians. Evangelicals are regenerated Christian believers who have experienced a life-changing relationship with God through faith in Jesus Christ as their Savior and Lord. They are men and women who are committed to the Bible as the revealed, inspired Word of God.

That biblical record describes the ascension of our risen Jesus and preserves the words of the "two men dressed in white" who spoke to Jesus' wonder-struck disciples:

> "Men of Galilee," they said, "why do you stand here looking into the sky? This same Jesus, who has been taken from you into heaven, will come back in the same way you have seen him go into heaven." (Acts 1:11)

We have also the revelation given to the apostle Paul, and his inspired counsel to the Thessalonian church:

> We believe that Jesus died and rose again and so we believe that God will bring with Jesus those who have fallen asleep in him. According to the Lord's own word, we tell you that we who are still alive, who are left till the coming of the Lord, will certainly not precede those who have fallen asleep. For the Lord himself will come down from heaven, with a loud command, with the voice of the archangel and with

the trumpet call of God, and the dead in Christ will rise first. After that, we who are still alive and are left will be caught up with them in the clouds to meet the Lord in the air. And so we will be with the Lord forever. Therefore encourage each other with these words. (1 Thessalonians 4:14–18)

Jesus could return soon

When it comes to the many details of Christian eschatology, we are not dogmatic and unbending. For instance, what I know about our promised heavenly home must be only a small and insignificant part of all that God has prepared for His children.

God has His own timing, and all of His plans are good plans for His children. There is an important point to make concerning God's timing in the case of Enoch. Enoch was a man of faith, a child of God. We could call him one of God's faithful few. God took him out of the earth and out of his race when the judgment of the Flood was not far away.

Jesus taught very clearly during His ministry that the Flood came on earth as a judgment for sin and ungodliness. When he was asked about the signs of His coming and the events of the future, Jesus said:

As it was in the days of Noah, so it will be at the coming of the Son of Man. For in the days before the flood, people were eating and drinking, marrying and giving in marriage, up to the day Noah entered the ark; and they knew nothing about what would happen until the flood came and took them all away. That is how it will be at the coming of the Son of Man. (Matthew 24:37–39)

All of us surely have moments when we wonder if we are seriously living in preparation for the coming of our Lord and for the eternity when we will be at home with Him. In our faith and trust, we know that God in His grace owns us and calls us His believing children, His saints. Yet, we do have times of discouragement concerning our shortcomings and failures.

The faith of Enoch continues to be an encouragement to walk with the King of heaven while we live down here. Then we know we will feel comfortable and at home when we get to heaven!

The facts are plainly spelled out. Enoch walked with God. He faced up to the devil and patiently bore the scoffing of those who lived like the devil. God honored his faith and took him into His divine presence forever.

I think we may draw the certain conclusion that when Enoch arrived in God's presence—raptured, translated, changed—he was completely at home, completely satisfied.

An important personal lesson

Now, here is one of the great personal lessons for us: Enoch was a spiritual rebuke to his own generation. He fought off the wiles and the temptations of the devil. He purposed within himself: "I will walk with God by faith even if that means that I must be detached from my generation."

Are you really detached from your generation because you resist the devil and walk in the fullness of the Holy Spirit?

Am I?

That is a very personal question, and we dare not try to answer it for each other.

Our generation in this world system claims that there is no personal devil, no enemy of our souls. Yet, all the while, Satan is busy. He is using a successful, age-old tactic with many people. He is assuring them in a variety of ways that there is no urgency in the matters of faith.

"Put off your decisions until a more favorable time," Satan says. "Do not make a decision until your situation eases!" The devil gambles on the odds that men and women will never heed God's warning that "Now is the accepted time."

"Put off a decision until you feel you are ready." That is the devil's urging to those who are lost. As a result, millions have waited. And in waiting, they have never come to God in repentance and faith.

A closing warning

In closing, I must add a warning. Enoch could have written a book on human loneliness. We must make our choices even as Enoch did. Enoch refused to walk in agreement with the ungodly multitude of his generation.

There is nothing as meaningless as a shout from a crowd. The crowd may give a big cheer, but no one ever seems to quite know what the shout means.

Believing Christians with true faith in God know very well the meaning of loneliness. In most ways, they are already detached from their generation.

Yet, in spite of the devil and the criticism of the crowd, they continue to serve their generation by doing the will of God.

I have heard stories of sheep in a flock blindly following leaders over the edge of a steep cliff. It seems that it is in the nature of sheep to follow the crowd. It is as though the word is passed along from one to another: "Don't be a dissenter! Don't try to be different! Just continue along with the crowd!" So they all go over the cliff, one after another—but they have stuck with the crowd!

Enoch determined that even if everyone in his generation was blindly moving toward the judgment of God, he would be the one man who refused to go over the cliff with the unbelievers. What did he do?

In faith Enoch detached himself from his generation. Then, by faith, he lived above all generations, pleasing to God.

The result? The life and testimony and victory of Enoch have become a benediction to all generations.

The warning? If we are satisfied to settle down and become weak victims amid the sins of our generation, we will die with our generation.

There is an alternative. If we will rise by faith above our generation, we, like Enoch, will prove to be a benediction to those who are yet to come!

Noah: Faith Does What God Asks

PEOPLE ALL AROUND US REMEMBER NOAH because he built a mammoth boat on a dry hillside—and they are still laughing at him. The Bible remembers Noah for his faith in God—and commends him for doing exactly what God told him to do.

If there were comics in Noah's day, they surely worked over the old man—building his big boat so far from water. While they were getting their laughs, they refused to believe that God had said to Noah: "I am going to put an end to all people, for the earth is filled with violence because of them" (Genesis 6:13). They refused to believe that God is sovereign.

The weight of the Bible is on the side of Noah's faith. "Noah," the Scriptures declare, "did everything just as God commanded him" (6:22). The New Testament measurement of Noah's faith is brief, but stirring and memorable:

> By faith Noah, when warned about things not yet seen, in holy fear built an ark to save his family. By his faith he condemned the world and became heir of the righteousness that comes by faith. (Hebrews 11:7)

Noah was not a popular figure in his day. But he was God's man in history's worst crisis, and he was faithful in the prophetic ministry God gave him.

Now, when we discuss Noah and the Flood, we must discuss sin and judgment and alarm—and none of these are topics likely to make any 20th-century person popular. But nevertheless we will find out where the Bible takes us as we review the faith and obedience of Noah.

Unlocking the lesson of Noah

There are some teachers in our churches who are strong on what they call "Bible analysis." They are always searching for the "key" to the book or the "key verse" of the chapter, or perhaps even the "key word" in a Bible verse.

Although it is helpful in Bible study to discern the variety in the sections and segments that compose the Scriptures, a "key" is something else. Personally, I do not think our Bible was formulated in that way. If you need to find a key and do not find it, the message remains locked in. That is not the way the Bible speaks to us and guides us.

It is often remarked that the Bible is really a love letter to us from God. Suppose a sailor is stationed somewhere in the western Pacific. He writes a tender, loving letter to his wife, at home with the children half a world away. When it arrives in the mail box, the sailor's wife quickly opens the envelope.

What is that wife's first thought as she begins to read? Is it, "I wonder if I am going to be able to find the key to the message in this letter"? Oh, no! That is not her thought at all. She reads with joy and blessing and satisfaction. She senses the love that authored the letter. She does not need a college degree to understand and absorb the message of every paragraph.

In considering Noah's faith, we do not have to search very far for understanding. The Bible gives us a straightforward message concerning Noah. It is simply. this: "Demonstrate your faith in God in your everyday life!"

It is evident that God did not say to Noah: "I am depending on you to hold the proper orthodox doctrines. Everything will be just fine if you stand up for the right doctrines!" No, that is not what God demanded of Noah. Yet we have many religiously inclined people in our day who hold to an illusion that the learning of doctrine is enough. They actually think that somehow they are better for having learned the doctrines of religion.

What actually did God ask Noah to do? Just this: to believe, to trust, to obey—to carry out His word. In essence, God said to Noah, "I want to demonstrate to the whole world that your faith is genuine and that I am a rewarder of those who believe Me and trust Me!"

Doctrine must be enfleshed

I have been impressed by a statement on Christian doctrine made by Martin Lloyd-Jones, the English preacher and writer, in a published article. The gist of his message was this: It is perilously close to being sinful for any person to learn doctrine for doctrine's sake. I agree with his conclusion that doctrine is always best when it is incarnated—when it is seen fleshed out in the lives of godly men and women.

Doctrine merely stated has no arms or legs, no tongue and no teeth. Standing alone, it has no purpose, no intentions, and it certainly carries no moral imperative.

Our God Himself appeared at His very best in the Incarnation, when He came into our world and lived in our flesh. What He had been trying to say to mortal man about Himself, He was now able to demonstrate in the person and life of Jesus, the Son of Man.

How can we best explain faith? Read the Bible account of Abraham—you will see faith in his life. How can we best explain courage? Read about Elijah and his challenge to the 400 prophets of Baal—you will find courage incarnated in a man. How can we best explain faithfulness? Turn to the life of Moses. Forgiveness? Turn to Joseph.

Now, what do we see in the life of Noah? Noah demonstrates many aspects of faith, but the particular emphasis is this: Faith pays heed to the warnings that come from God.

In the kind of world in which we live, men and women can easily come to the conclusion that so many alarms are false alarms that there is really no need to be concerned. But when God sounds a loud and commanding alarm, we should listen and exercise concern. When God said to Noah, "I will destroy man, whom I have created, from the face of the earth," Noah believed God and acted in the light of the serious nature of that alarm.

When God warns a nation or a city, a church or a person, it is a grievous sin to ignore such warning. In conservative Christianity, we believe that the Christian message does indeed contain an element of alarm. Not all Christians believe this. Some have been taught that the Christian gospel is "good news" exclusively. The only way some people try to explain the full meaning of the Christian gospel is to quote one verse: "Believe in the Lord Jesus, and you will be saved" (Acts 16:31). That is it! That is all there is to it, they say.

The positive suggests the negative

But I want to mention something here about the use of language. It is impossible to make certain definite statements without bringing to mind that which is exactly the opposite. If I should say, for example, "I was introduced to one of the largest men I have ever met," I am making a comparison in my mind. I try to describe the man as large, and I cannot do that without having also a small man in my mind. If a small man did not exist, I could not be describing the other man as large.

So when the Scriptures admonish us to believe in the Lord Jesus Christ to be saved, there comes to our minds the fact of mankind's lost condition. Why should I have to believe in Christ to be saved? Because I am lost. Because I am a sinner. Because I have believed the devil and all of his works unto near damnation! I am alienated from God.

Even in John 3:16, the most beautiful and rose-colored verse of all, there is an element of alarm sounding continually for the lost: "For God so loved the world that he gave his one and only Son, that whoever believes in him shall not perish but have eternal life." Salvation is there, yes! But the word *perish* is plainly there, too. And the alarming lost condition of the human race is there.

This is the basic reality of our faith – the reality of believing and trusting. The Christian gospel always has been and must continue to be a gospel of alarm. The Christian gospel cannot always be a gospel of honey and sweetness! It follows that there is a kind of faith that responds, that believes in the soundness of a warning that comes from God.

The gospel message is a gospel of hope and good news to those who respond and believe. But the gospel message is starkly plain to those who do not believe. "Whoever does not believe stands condemned already because he has not believed in the name of God's one and only Son" (John 3:18).

Noah accepted the reality of God's warning of judgment to come. He demonstrated his faith by acknowledging that God's way is best and the best of all courses of action.

But why did Noah "fear"?

Now, some voice a negative reaction to the expression in Hebrews that declares Noah was moved by a "holy fear" to do all God had commanded. The English language does not always give us a proper perspective of the word *fear*.

If we are familiar with the Bible and the many godly men and women who have trusted the Lord, we know that holy fear is a kind of faith closely associated with high moral wisdom. It can only be the part of wisdom for a human being to fear irrecoverable spiritual loss. It is a wise kind of fear that is willing to consider the meaning of permanent and eternal separation from God, the source of all good.

Noah demonstrated a high quality of human wisdom as well as spiritual concern when he was moved to trust God and His word. Noah did not argue about his rights. He did not argue about God's assessment of man's nature and man's violence. He did not argue about God's course of action.

Noah's high regard for God's person was intermingled with his own reverent faith and holy fear. His knowledge of God was firsthand and personal. God had revealed Himself, and Noah said, "I will trust, I will follow, I will believe!"

Because Noah's fear was a holy fear, he was moved to prepare for the acts of God that were to follow. Noah's fear moved him. It is that simple and that significant. Nothing but the will of God was of any consequence to him.

I must note here a modern method of dealing with human fear, human guilt, human sin. Psychology is somewhere at the center of it. I speak of the expansion in our day of the old Greek idea that realistic drama could be utilized as a moral catharsis. The Greek authors said they wrote all of the harshness and terror, anguish and sorrow into their famed plays so those in the audience could experience the complete sweep of human emotions. Men and women were supposed to be able to live through it all by watching the portrayal by someone else.

I have never believed that the Greeks succeeded in bringing their idea to any desired moral fruition. In our day, however, the concept is still advocated. It is being carried out to a ridiculous extreme.

Many people who make up our television and

theater audiences, who may have never shed a real tear for any real person, will actually weep over the emotional trials and tribulations of the TV and movie actors. A moral catharsis, the Greeks said. Get yourself so identified with some imaginary character that you can live out all of your emotions. Then you will experience a kind of purification.

You will experience nothing of the kind!

What will happen is that you will become an artificial zombie! You will get so wrapped up in your feelings for what is unreal and artificial that you will never have right feelings of concern for what is real and true.

Noah faced reality

That may sound like it is far and remote from Noah's faith, but there is a connection. Noah was moved—but he was on no emotional binge. He was not moved by depraved, guilty human fear. He was moved by the personal knowledge of a revelation from a holy and sovereign God.

When something unusual happens to us, we exclaim, "That is unreal!" Noah had word from the Lord. He said: "This is real! I know this is real! It is the better part of wisdom for me to do just what God has commanded!"

Many people around us are moved by their emotions, but they are not moved enough to do anything that matters. They are not happy until they have had "a good cry." I have met some of them. They can cry at the drop of a handkerchief. Then, just as suddenly, the tears are gone, and they look pleased, saying they feel "so much better."

I cannot keep up with that kind of temperament

or personality. I must confess it nearly kills me to cry in public. I am not one of the weepy kind. My tears are very far down in the well. If anything is powerful enough to get them to the surface, I am undergoing some deep and demanding experience within my being.

But we should be moved and we should be stirred about eternal realities. Noah was moved—and he moved on to do that which was right and important.

I once heard a very fine speaker, an effective preacher, describe what he had found in the emotional responses of an audience. He said he had told the story of a faithful old sheep dog. In the midst of a great storm, the herder knew that 11 young lambs were missing. Once, twice, three times he sent Old Shep, the dog, out for the missing lambs. And again and again, until the weary but faithful dog had returned with 10 of the lambs.

Once again the master took Old Shep to the door. "One more, Shep, one more," he said. "Bring him in!" The dog, utterly exhausted, went out into the storm again. Much later he returned, bearing the missing lamb. The old dog slowly placed the weak, wet lamb on the floor, then slumped to the floor himself.

As the shepherd finished caring for the stray lamb, he turned to Old Shep to express his gratitude. But it was too late. Shep was dead. The faithful dog had given his all to rescue the lambs.

But reality failed to stir them

The preacher who was describing his telling of the story said his audience was in tears as he finished. To that audience, then, he made the gospel application, deliberately and intentionally. He told of the faithfulness of the Son of Man as He was led to Calvary. He described the kind of love that motivated Jesus to die on Calvary's cross.

"I painted the picture of Jesus as vividly as I could," said the preacher in recounting the experience. "I let the Savior hang there for men and women to see."

And what was the result? "An obvious look of stony indifference came over those people," the preacher concluded. "They had been moved by the story of the faithful dog. They had been moved to tears. But the Savior's dying on the cross? They had heard that before—and they were no longer stirred by it."

Yes, Noah had feelings. Noah was stirred. But he did not stand still, wondering and debating. He was moved to face the consequences in the glare of an unbelieving and godless generation.

Noah went out to the hillside and began the long, weary task of building the ark. He constructed it exactly to the pattern God had given him. He condemned the world in its unbelief. He became heir to the righteousness that is by faith.

What would Noah say to you if he could come and counsel you today concerning your faith? I know what he would say—and I think you know, too.

"When you hear the truth," Noah would say, "whenever you hear God's truth, God's Word, you will go either in the direction you are moved, or you will just wait. If you wait, you will find that the next time you hear the truth, it will not move you quite as much. The next time, it will move you less, and the time will come when that truth will not move you at all!"

Then Noah would probably finish his counsel, saying, "If I had refused the very first time to go out and build the ark, God might have spoken again. But each time it would have been a little easier to say, 'No, Lord, I don't think I am going to do it.' Soon I would be able to disregard completely the alarm that God was sounding!"

Do not disregard the warning!

We have to confess that there is a distressing kind of brazen unbelief all around us. Because they are completely without fear of God, men and women in our generation are paying little heed to any of God's warning signals.

As a youngster I was a farm boy, and I came to recognize that birds and animals had their own methods of communication particularly when danger or harm were near. There were always some hungry crows flying around, and they communicated in their own ways. But only one of their sharp cries was the cry of alarm, the urgent warning of danger.

Some of the crows were brave enough to land in the field and pick away at the corn. But they had an advance and a rear guard—wily old crows perched on the stubby branch of a nearby tree, or on a post. Their instincts warned them of the farmers with their rifles who never gave up in their contest with the greedy crows. One man on the edge of the field brought that warning cry from the crow in the tree—and all of the crows took off as one, escaping to their places of safety.

Here is my point. It would have been a very foolish crow that would have belittled the alarm, that would have lingered for one more kernel of corn. He might have rejected his bird instinct and declared, "I am staying! I am not going to be stampeded." But you know what would happen. The farmer with the rifle would blow out his poor little bird brain and that would be the end of him. He had heard the warning—it was up to him to heed it.

I also learned the lesson of the little chicks—an easy prey for the hawks overhead. Sometimes before we could even see the hawk we could hear its high-pitched cry—a piercing whistle-like sound. Mother hen also heard it, and she would use her own special cluck-cluck of warning. Her chicks would scamper to her side and soon she had them all tucked away safely under her feathers. Those chicks did not lose any time debating the value of an alarm. They responded quickly and were safe from the danger overhead.

There is such a thing as faith that believes in the soundness of a warning. There is a faith that is not ashamed to move in the direction of the ark of safety.

Noah is an everlasting example. May God give us ears to hear and hearts to obey!

4

Faith Answers When God Calls

THERE HAVE ALWAYS BEEN outright, vocal critics of the Bible. Among them are those who try to generate sympathy for Old Testament Abraham.

These insist that Abraham was comfortable and well adjusted in Ur of the Chaldees, surrounded by relatives and friends. Probably he had his own business. He may have been about eligible for Social Security. He had stature in the community and status with his neighbors.

Into that happy, successful situation, a spoil-sport God, with utter disdain for Abraham's personal feelings, called him to a nomadic, isolated existence.

But the critics have failed to see the most important element in God's approach to Abraham. The living God made an almost incredible offer to the patriarch: "I want to be your Friend, and I want you to be My friend!"

The man or woman who by faith is a friend of God has lost nothing but sin and guilt. He or she has come into an eternal kingdom that assures everything that is good, forever and ever!

I want to make here a case for faith. The writer of

the Letter to the Hebrews gives us a summary look at Abraham and at the nature of his faith:

> By faith Abraham, when called to go to a place he would later receive as his inheritance, obeyed and went, even though he did not know where he was going. By faith he made his home in the promised land like a stranger in a foreign country; he lived in tents, as did Isaac and Jacob, who were heirs with him of the same promise. For he was looking forward to the city with foundations, whose architect and builder is God. (Hebrews 11:8–10)

I have discovered that if I want to learn more about God and faith and righteousness, it is profitable to think deeply about Abraham. I have tried to decide which were the most critical moments and the most important events in his life.

The single most critical, most important time in Abraham's life was when he heard and answered God's call.

Life's most important decision

Some people consider the hour of physical birth, when we begin to breathe and live and function as unique people within the human race, as the most important moment in life. Others mark their marriage as the most meaningful lifetime decision. But many, many have testified to the great importance of their spiritual decision—the act of faith whereby they committed themselves and their entire futures to God.

Undoubtedly (as I said) Abraham's single, most important moment was when God unexpectedly and dramatically revealed Himself to him and called him to be a pilgrim. So it was that, when he was called, Abraham by faith obeyed and went, even though he did not know where he was going.

We have all wondered at times about the method or methods God may have used to get through to Abraham. Do you suppose that Abraham had his own quiet times and considered the possibility of an unseen domain beyond the world he knew? Although Abraham did not have the privileges in the grace of God that we have, I am sure he was not afraid to think for himself—perhaps even about the mysteries of creation and life.

We do not know how much preparation Abraham had to make within his own soul to be ready for a direct revelation from God. I for one am perfectly satisfied to leave that theological question to the Calvinists and the Arminians!

In my own contemplations, though, I have found great comfort in the doctrine of prevenient grace. Prevenient grace, simply stated, is the belief that before a sinful man or woman can seek God, God must first have sought the man or woman.

God has told us in many ways that He is a person. In making Himself known to us, He uses the familiar pattern of personality. He is able to communicate with us through the channels of our minds, our wills and our emotions.

If we hold to our belief that men and women were originally created in the image of God, we also must believe that there resides within our beings a capacity to know God. That is why Jesus spoke to Nicodemus about an invisible but transforming new birth from above!

The response must be ours

We are humans, and we confess that we do not know all of God's ways. We do not know the steps of searching and seeking that brought about the actual friendship between God and Abraham. Perhaps we can glimpse a clue in the confession of Augustine: "Thou madest us for Thyself, and our heart is restless, until it repose in Thee!"

We discern that a loving Personality dominates the Bible, walking among the trees in the Garden of Eden and breathing fragrance over every scene. Always a living Person is present, speaking, pleading, loving and manifesting Himself whenever and wherever His people are responsive and receptive.

If God had not in His own way first moved toward Abraham, Abraham would never have moved toward God. I do believe that! I also believe, however, that if Abraham had been insensitive, he would never have heard God's voice calling him. That was indeed the critical moment in the life of Abraham. Abraham was a man. It is well known that many men have set their jaws and stubbornly clenched their fists as they confidently assured themselves, "I am self-sufficient! I will not bow to this business of religion!"

If Abraham had rejected God's overtures, he would have returned to making bigger and better idols for men and women intent on choosing their own brand of deity. And you can mark this down, too: If Abraham had refused the calling of God, the whole history of the world would have been vastly different, and different for the worse.

The Bible record of God's calling people is varied,

yet always consistent. Moses was alone with his sheep in the desert when God said, "I have heard the cry of my people. I want you to go to Pharaoh and say, 'Let my people go.'" Moses tried to squirm out of that call. But the hand of God had been laid on him and he could not escape.

Jacob also was alone in the wilderness. He was running away from a bad situation at home. He had a night vision of heavenly angels ascending and descending, and there God spoke to him. God called him. And through that call Jacob the cheat became Israel, a prince with God.

We need to get quiet

The gospel invitation is offered to one and all, but many are too preoccupied to hear or heed. They never allow God's call to become a reason for decision. Their relationship with God never becomes a personal encounter. As a result, they live out their entire lives insisting that they never heard any call from God.

The answer to that is plain. God has been trying to get through to them, but their line is always busy! They are engrossed in a host of worldly pursuits.

In our activistic, achievement-oriented era, there is a prevailing notion that no person really amounts to anything if he or she cannot be described as a "go-getter." The go-getter is the person who never allows himself or herself to be quiet or still—not even for a minute. He or she is our ever-ready nominee to get things done. Given time, he or she will turn the world upside down.

But it is surely necessary for us to have times when we stop what we are doing and think for a season. I try to practice the art of quietness often, for there is not a person alive who can meditate while involved in the non-stop, hundred-mile-an-hour pace of the ambitious go-getter.

The Quakers had many fine ideas about life, and there is a story from them that illustrates the point I am trying to make. It concerns a conversation between Samuel Taylor Coleridge and a Quaker woman he had met. Maybe Coleridge was boasting a bit, but he told the woman how he had arranged the use of time so he would have no wasted hours. He said he memorized Greek while dressing and during breakfast. He went on with his list of other mental activities—making notes, reading, writing, formulating thoughts and ideas—until bedtime.

The Quaker listened unimpressed. When Coleridge was finished with his explanation, she asked him a simple, searching question: "My friend, when dost thee think?"

God is having a difficult time getting through to us because we are a fast-paced generation. We seem to have no time for contemplation. We have no time to answer God when He calls.

When the important matters of the soul are at stake, the most useful thing we can do is to do nothing, even if only for a short time. There are times when we can go the fastest by not going at all. We can go farthest by standing still for a while.

Then, too, we can talk the loudest by not saying a word. We will not be taking the Lord by surprise; He will speak *His* message.

Abraham was listening

Abraham was listening. He was probably alone somewhere when God spoke to him. In our day, we are so socially minded that we cannot endure being alone. People say they are in misery if they are alone.

I knew of a young man who was hospitalized and forced to lie quietly for a time. He implored his father, "Dad, bring my record player or something to keep me busy. Otherwise I just have to lie here and think." Then he added his own commentary on the nature of his personal life, "And it is hell to think."

If we do not give God a listening ear, we will miss His best for our lives. He wants to bring us into the right place, the best place for His will in us to be accomplished.

For Abraham, Ur of the Chaldees was not the right place. The eternal God had plans for something far better. In order for Abraham to be known as "the friend of God" and "the father of the faithful," he had to go out from the place that held him. Either he would act in faith, going against the voice of reason, or he would respond, "I can be satisfied to think that all gods and all religions and all worship are pretty much alike and all lead to the same conclusion!"

Abraham made his choice, and by faith he demonstrated that there is a difference in following a God and Creator who lives eternally.

The world around us wants to put us in the same restrictive straitjacket that would have kept Abraham in Ur of the Chaldees. "We will talk to you about religion" is the seemingly kindly offer people give us today. But then they add the disclaimer: "Just do not make religion personal."

"Christianity is all right," they assure us, "if you are willing to be tolerant and not try to make something exclusive of your Christian faith." Most people seem to have come to terms with an acceptance of religion if it does not have the cross of Christ within it.

But as soon as you begin to quote the words of Jesus and the Scriptures that declare there is only one mediator between God and mankind, as soon as you insist that Christ has given us the only way to God through His death and atonement, you are dead!

"That is bigoted, narrow dogmatism," they shout. "No more dialogue with you! You have no place on a panel where we are cooperatively interested in intellectual ferment!"

I lived on the farm long enough to know what happens when things are allowed to ferment. If that is what the modern intellectuals are trying to achieve, I am glad I have never had time to take part in their religious panel discussions! They have predetermined to agree only upon religious tenets that bring no offense to anyone.

But when God calls out men and women, their faith will be an offense to the world. It was so in Abraham's day, and it is so in our day.

God calls us *out* and *into*

But there is in Abraham's life another profound truth about the call of God. God does not just call us out, period. He is completely faithful to call us into something better!

I do not consider that Christian believers are fully on the right track when they proclaim, "We are separated! We have come out! We are paying the price! We are trying to endure! Pray for us that we can stick it out to the end!"

In his faith, Abraham was against idolatry and idol-making, but that was not his crusade. Because of his faith, God led him into a promised land, into possessions and into the lineage that brought forth the Messiah. The call of God is always to something better. Keep that in mind.

God calls us into the joys and reality of eternal life. He calls us into purity of life and spirit, so that we may acceptably walk with Him. He calls us into a life of service and usefulness that brings glory to Himself as our God. He calls us into the sweetest fellowship possible on this earth—the fellowship of the family of God!

I hope I never hear any Christian bragging even a little bit about what he or she gave up and how much it cost him or her to answer the call of God. Anything that we were or any abilities that we possessed were as nothing compared to what God has called us into as His believing children.

Why is it so difficult in our churches for us to be honest about our lives and our condition as sinners alienated from God? We did not give up anything when God in His love and mercy called us unto Himself and into the blessings of grace and forgiveness and peace.

I have been asked more than once what I gave up when I was converted and became a believing child of God. I was a young man, and I well remember that I gave up the hot and smelly rubber factory. I was making tires for an hourly wage, and I gave that up to follow Christ's call into Christian ministry and service.

As a youth I was scared of life and I was scared of death—and I gave that up. I was miserable and glum and unfulfilled—and I gave that up. I had selfish earthly and material ambitions that I could never have achieved—and I gave them up.

That forms the outline of the worthless things that I gave up. And I soon discovered that in Jesus Christ, God had given me everything that is worthwhile.

God gives us far more

If God takes away from us the old, wrinkled, beat-up dollar bill we have clutched so desperately, it is only because He wants to exchange it for the whole Federal mint, the entire treasury! He is saying to us, "I have in store for you all the resources of heaven. Help yourself!"

If Abraham had ever grumbled to the Lord about leaving the beggarly idols of Ur, God would have let him go back. We are *free* to do the will of God, but God never makes us His unwilling prisoners. God called Abraham out, God gave him the promised land and God said, "Abraham, from among your posterity will come the Messiah in the fullness of time!"

This is the gracious reason why we should tell people everywhere to hear and heed the call of God—so He can lead them into everything that is good and blessed and worthwhile.

We are called to share these matters of truth and life with a wider circle than we sometimes care to admit. On occasion someone has advised me not to accept preaching engagements with non-fundamentalist groups. A so-called liberal church invited me to speak for nearly a week at a Bible conference in Minnesota. They wanted to hear Bible exposition on the baptism of the Holy Spirit. When this was announced, I soon had a letter from a Christian brother warning me against going. "Don't you know that they are just using you?" he asked.

My reply was that I expected *God* to use me, for I intended to glorify Him—Father, Son and Holy Spirit! I intended to tell that conference of ministers and laypeople what God the Holy Spirit can do in the lives of those who will answer His call.

Let me repeat: God wants to call us out into a more abundant and fruitful Christian life than we have ever known!

The late evangelist "Uncle Bud" Robinson well summarized all I have said. "Abraham went out not knowing where he was going," Uncle Bud said, "but he knew Who he was going with!"

Abraham was interested in a dwelling place that would never decay. He looked forward in faith to a city with eternal foundations, whose builder and maker is God. It is important to us that our Lord Jesus Christ confirmed Abraham's choice when He told the Jews, "Abraham saw my day, and was glad!"

Abraham in faith dedicated himself to eternal things. No writer needs to spend time making a case for that. The long, glory-studded history of faithful Abraham is its own justification.

In simplest terms, God blesses anyone and everyone who will believe and trust and obey. And He speaks to everyone of us with a heavenly call.

If we are genuinely and irrevocably committed to our Lord Jesus Christ, if we are willing to follow Him at any cost, we dare to pray, "Oh God, make me like Abraham in faith and obedience, with spiritual vision of the eternity to come!"

Faith Values the Pilgrim Journey

Y OU ARE A CHRISTIAN. THAT you admit. You go to church nearly every Sunday. "Just ask the minister; he will confirm it."

You have been working and earning, getting and spending, and now you are enjoying the creature comforts known to modern human beings in this land.

You bristle a little and ask, "Is there anything wrong with being comfortable?"

Let me answer in this way: If you are a Christian and you are comfortably "at home" in Chicago or Toronto, in Iowa or Alberta—or any other address on planet earth—the signs are evident that you are in spiritual trouble.

The spiritual equation reads like this: The greater your contentment with your daily circumstances in this world, the greater your defection from the ranks of God's pilgrims en route to a city whose architect and builder is God Himself!

The writer of the Letter to the Hebrews centuries ago described the long-range faith of the many victorious pilgrims who could never really feel at home in this world:

All these people were still living by faith when they died. They did not receive the things promised; they only saw them and welcomed them from a distance. And they admitted that they were aliens and strangers on earth. People who say such things show that they are looking for a country of their own. If they had been thinking of the country they had left, they would have had opportunity to return. Instead, they were longing for a better country—a heavenly one. Therefore God is not ashamed to be called their God, for he has prepared a city for them. (Hebrews 11:13–16)

One of the most telling indictments against many of us who comprise our Christian churches today is the almost complete acceptance of the contemporary scene as our permanent home. We say that we are followers of Christ, but we have already settled down and we are comfortably at home. We are satisfied to be natives and citizens of this world's society—we are no longer "aliens and strangers."

If we can feel that we have put down our roots in this present world, if we have a true sense of belonging, then our Lord still has much to teach us about faith and attachment to our Savior.

Our citizenship is in heaven

The apostle Paul emphasized an important New Testament teaching concerning our true citizenship as believing Christians when he declared:

Our citizenship is in heaven. And we eagerly await a Savior from there, the Lord Jesus Christ, who, by the power that enables him to bring everything under his control, will transform our lowly bodies so that they will be like his glorious body. (Philippians 3:20–21)

Those are not just comforting words to be recited at the graveside. They are words of truth and hope for aliens and strangers, walking by faith on this earth, who know that their true citizenship is in heaven.

We are speaking of genuine, abiding faith in God. And I want to note with you an interesting observation. In Hebrews 11 there are three prepositions used with the word *faith*. Each has something to do with our Christian pilgrimage.

How did God's heroes live? How did they meet temptations and sufferings? How did they die? Everything was "by faith," "through faith" or "in faith."

Throughout the ages, this has been the pattern of God's methodology for His faithful men and women. We do certain things *by* faith. We accomplish certain things *through* faith. Some things we do *in* faith, trusting and believing even in dark times. I emphasize these prepositions here as a contrast to the philosophies of the worldlings around us—those who tell us that they live and operate "on faith."

All adult my life I have been a minister in The Christian and Missionary Alliance. When I started out, many of the Alliance pastors did not receive a regular weekly salary. Rather, they lived "by faith." Members of their congregations would contribute a part of their weekly tithes and offerings direct to their minister's support. Whatever they gave, that the pastor had as his income. And so these ministers lived "by faith" without a fixed remuneration.

Living *by* faith versus living *on* faith

Often members of the group would comment that their pastor was "living *on* faith." Some of the pastors were sure their people knew only the one preposition—living "on" faith. It was reported by one of the early evangelists that an Alliance woman was critical of her pastor for buying a piece of beefsteak "when everyone knows that he is living on faith." Apparently they thought that because the pastor was willing to live *by* faith he could exist *on* faith.

A thousand times no! None of us should be living *on* faith, for if we rest *on* faith we have a complete misunderstanding of what faith is. The purpose of faith is to get us to rest completely on *God*—on God Himself!

It is only *by* faith that we can rest on God. It is *through* faith that we can trust the promises of God. It is *in* faith that we can daily live our lives in dependence upon God, His Word and His promises.

These are the Christian contrasts to the worldly philosophy of human activity and presumption *on* faith. "Just go ahead bravely on faith. Never say die!"—that is the self-courageous attitude of this world.

"Never say die!" But then they die.

"You can if you will—it is all up to you," is the world's refrain. "He who thinks he can, can!"

Since I have been a Christian, I have had a negative reaction to that kind of human psychology. I do not mind saying that my favorite hymns are not those that exhort me to rise up, bare my chest to the elements, flex my biceps and tell the world where to get off. That is not my philosophy because it would put my confidence in the wrong place. If my faith, my belief, my confidence are in myself, then they cannot at the same time be resting in God.

The Bible tells us to believe in God and to put our trust in Him. It warns us against having any confidence in the flesh. So I do not want some voice exhorting me to "Rise up, O man of God, go forth to face the foe"—and all of that. I would rather go to the place of prayer, meet God there and then let Him face the world for me.

To meet the kinds of temptations and enemies confronting us, it is not enough for us to stick out our chins, inflate our chests and mutter the old refrain, "Never say die!" We do not operate *on* faith; rather, we rest our case completely on God. Then our experiences proceed *by* faith, *through* faith and *in* faith. That is the way victory comes, because our victory must be God's victory first!

Two kinds of faith

I see two kinds of faith in these verses from Hebrews 11. The more important, by far, is the long-range, unchanging faith in God's person and in God's plan no matter how long His plan takes. I call this long-range faith. It is the quality of being able to trust God far into the future.

The other kind of faith is short-range. It is the faith of the beginner, the eager new believer who wants everything to happen *now!* These new creations in Christ Jesus have confessed their faith in

Him Christ and have sensed the joy of being forgiven for their sins. They are likely to be taken up
with today's blessings, today's provision, today's
expectations. As yet, they know little of persecution, temptations, the wiles of the devil, the loneliness of the minority.

So far, their faith in God is short-range, immedi-
ate. They have not yet heard of all those heroes of
faith who believed, persevered, suffered, clung to
all of God's promises and died in faith not having
seen the fulfillment of God's great plan.

Generally in our Christian circles when we talk
about the promises of God, we refer to God's im-
mediate provision and to blessings for our present
needs. But in effect, Christ has said to us, "I have a
long-range plan for you! I am asking you to forsake
all for Me, transfer every allegiance to Me, trust
completely in Me. Then in the day of My triumph
and vindication, you will triumph with Me. When I
come into My ultimate glory, you will share in that
glory!"

Pilgrims and strangers

Let me tell you something that is very evident in
God's dealings with us. Anyone who truly knows
the demands of faith, anyone who is genuinely
committed to the Christian life is both a pilgrim
and a stranger in this world. (I like that term *pilgrim*, used in some translations, better than *alien*,
so I will use it.)

The words *pilgrim* and *stranger* are synonymous,
yet they are not identical. A pilgrim is generally a
religious traveler who is determined to visit some
holy place. History tells us about people making

pilgrimages. Many individuals and many groups endured hardships and sufferings in order to reach the places on earth that they considered sacred.

Pilgrims are never pictured as seeking some commercial gain. They are intent upon a higher motive, and they keep traveling and seeking because they have not yet found that place they can call home.

Simply, pilgrims who are still pilgrims have not arrived at that place to which they are going. They are still moving toward their objective.

What, then, is a stranger? A stranger is one who has found a place of residence but who cannot truly consider himself or herself a part of the new culture. He or she may be of another race and speak a different language. The culture that surrounds him or her is completely different from that which he or she has known.

If we are genuine, committed Christians, intent upon walking by faith with our Lord Jesus Christ, then we are continually confessing that we are pilgrims and that we are strangers!

The Holy Spirit, who is the real author of this Letter to the Hebrews, uses the terms *pilgrims* and *strangers* to remind the early Christians that they were not yet at their final home.

The message still reads the same today. Christian pilgrims are journeying by faith from an old city that is cursed and under threat of judgment to a blessed and celestial city where dwells Immanuel!

As Christian pilgrims and strangers, we are never borne along by force or compulsion. We remain free moral agents. We have not been squeezed or coerced into a profession of faith. Christ has chosen us, and we have followed Him gladly and freely.

Why do I speak of that here? Because the writer to the Hebrews has told us that the heroes of faith, the pilgrims and strangers of old, could have turned back to their native city and home. Abraham could have gone back. If he had found that he was longing for Ur of the Chaldees and that his pilgrimage with God was no longer his soul's desire, he could have turned around and said, "I am going back!"

Not everyone follows through

In the New Testament, that man described as a rich young ruler in the national and religious life of Israel came to Jesus to inquire about faith and choice. Jesus said to him, "Leave all; become a pilgrim and follow Me!"

That young man was free to choose, free to believe, free to follow the Son of Man. But he turned back. He walked away. There is nothing in the New Testament record to indicate that Jesus ever came in contact with him again.

Demas was a Christian brother in the company of the apostle Paul. With Luke, he was actually linked as a loyal prison companion of Paul in Rome. Yet when Paul wrote his final letter from prison, he regretfully reported to Timothy, "Demas, because he loved this world, has deserted me." That is the last we hear of Demas in the New Testament record.

In this life, we will never have a complete record of pilgrims who became weary and discouraged and decided to turn back.

I am not seeking to raise any theological controversy here. I think there are those who may be described as "borderline Christians." We might well ask them, "Will you also go back? Do you think your treasure is still lying back there in some of your old practices and pleasures?" The truth is that none of us can ever really go back to yesterday. It has crumbled and is gone!

Some, perhaps like Demas, are tempted to turn back for money or business or gain. But what good is money when the doctor announces, "Your cancer is far advanced. You have only a short time to live"?

Others are tempted to turn back by their memories of pleasures and "good times" with worldly and sinful friends. I remember a young man who was with us for a while in our fellowship in Chicago. He was frank about it—he told me that he was not really happy with us. He said he was looking for a church where dancing was offered as a social attraction.

Our Lord Jesus Christ asks us to believe, to trust, to follow. My only judgment of those who turn back, those who no longer are pilgrims in the way, is the sad knowledge that they will find that the enemy of their souls has sold them out, deceived them, embittered them.

Certainly Saul of Tarsus became a pilgrim when he met the Lord on the road to Damascus. Saul the persecutor became Paul the apostle. Later he wrote with confidence concerning the exact location of his life's lasting treasure:

> Of this gospel I was appointed a herald and an apostle and a teacher. That is why I am suffering as I am. Yet I am not ashamed, because I know whom I have believed, and am convinced

that he is able to guard what I have entrusted to him for that day. (2 Timothy 1:11–12)

Paul, the pilgrim, knew that the Lord had his treasure—and that He would hold it for him. If Paul had gone back, what treasure would he claim throughout eternity?

Our identification is with Jesus

We who are involved in the upward gaze of this long-range faith identify ourselves with Jesus Christ forever! We are satisfied that God is at work. We are satisfied to be misunderstood for Christ's sake. We are willing to be treated as the minority, for the people of God are always in the minority in this earthly context.

Our true identity is with Jesus Christ, our Savior and Lord. We have taken His cause as our cause. We have taken His way as our way. We have taken His place as our place. We have taken His future as our future. We have taken His life as our life. We have taken the long look of faith to the day of His triumph, and we know it will be our triumph as well.

Let me remind you again of the nature of our earthly pilgrimage in the example set by the saintly Samuel Rutherford. His faith shone brightly in one of Scotland's crisis times.

Rutherford had refused to bow to the demands and strictures of the powerful leaders of the time. He was exiled by the state church, driven from his pastorate and the flock of God. His religious and political enemies finally dispatched a summons, setting the date for him to appear before their tribunal and face the charges of opposing and ignoring the state church.

Already advanced in years and knowing the illness that was about to claim his mortal life, Rutherford answered the summons with one of the most victorious letters ever written:

> I have received your summons. However, I have received a higher summons, which will be honored before yours. When the day set for me to appear before you comes, I will already be in yonder land where few kings and great men ever come.

Men and women committed to long-range faith can die with blessing and satisfaction even if they have not received the fulfillment of the promises. They have confessed themselves to be strangers and pilgrims on the earth. Their waiting is blessed because it is a waiting on God.

The Bible tells us that one of these days Jesus Christ, our Prince-Leader and Elder Brother, will return to reign on earth. He whose name is the Word of God will appear. The nations of this world will be called into account. The righteous Judge will separate the sheep from the goats.

By faith we have the assurance of God's favor and welcome in that wonderful hour when Jesus returns. It will be a glad day for the pilgrims—the pilgrims of eternity—their eyes fixed on heaven above.

That is the long-range kind of faith. Let us humbly, confidently ask God for it!

6

Faith Is Finding God for Ourselves

G OD IS NOT LOOKING for carbon copies of Abraham to believe Him and obey Him in this 20th century. He is not looking for carbon copies of Enoch, or Noah, or Moses, or David.

God is looking for people exactly like you and me. The old heroes of faith named in the 11th chapter of Hebrews have long ago gone to their reward, as the writer has reminded us:

> And what more shall I say? I do not have time to tell about Gideon, Barak, Samson, Jephthah, David, Samuel and the prophets. . . . They were stoned; they were sawed in two; they were put to death by the sword. They went about in sheepskins and goatskins, destitute, persecuted and mistreated—the world was not worthy of them. . . . These were all commended for their faith, yet none of them received what had been promised. God had planned something better for us so that only together with us would they be made perfect. (Hebrews 11: 32, 37–40)

It is plain to see from this text that God had us in

His heart and in His thoughts. Even as the Old Testament saints were passing on to be forever with the God they loved, God had us in mind, too. Those heroes of the faith died, but God did not die with them. The eternal character of God has never changed and it never will. God continues to be God. He continues to be in control throughout His universe. He assures us He is the God of the living. He is still yearning, loving, calling men and women everywhere. He is still gladly responding to the prayers of His believing people. Best of all, He is still seeking and wooing those of our day who are ready and willing to become His new heroes in the faith!

God has a design for each of us

I wonder if we are consistently holding to this assurance of God's presence and God's blessing in our Christian churches today. God *does* want to speak to all of us who will listen! I repeat: God is not looking for an exact replica of Abraham or Noah or David. He wants to bless, equip and use our individuality—every one of us who by faith make up His believing people in our own generation.

You cannot study the Book of Hebrews long without discovering that faith in God is neither an ordinary nor an imaginary quality. Godly faith is dynamic and powerful! The accomplishments of faith are rightfully attributed only to God, of course. But it is satisfying to know that the people He blesses and uses may be as different in personality as night is from day.

This is an important lesson for us to learn. God

does not intend that we who believe and trust Him shall all be alike—all poured into the same mold. No! It is actually one of the snares of Christian experience to think that we must copy one another.

Each one of us is different

God knew very well what He was doing when He created us to differ in personality, temperament and disposition. It has been well demonstrated that variety is the very hallmark of God's creation throughout the universe.

As humans, we do not understand how it can be, but biologists tells us they can examine thousands upon thousands of leaves in the forest and never find two exactly alike! In the Chicago church where I ministered for many years, we had identical twins—Irene and Ilene. We watched them grow and develop. Although they were called identical, they exhibited traits and expressions that were different. For that reason, most of us could tell them apart and call them by their right names.

We have come to realize and accept the fact that there are no two people exactly, identically alike in our world. And the point I am making is that God, the all-knowing divine artist, has formed each one of us out of His inexhaustible variety. He works in His wisdom and love to bless and honor the many differences—as well as the similarities—in men and women.

God accepts us no matter where we fall within the range of varying human personalities. He desires to manifest Himself to us and through us, no matter how different we may be. May I give you an illustration?

When the time comes around for the annual decorating of your Christmas tree, you get out the string or strings of lights that have been carefully packed since the year before. You wrap those lights as artistically as possible around your tree. You make sure you have a good mixture of red, green, yellow, blue and maybe white lights.

It is not likely you ever stop to worry whether you need more than one kind of electricity to light the bulbs of different colors. The same power, the same amount of power flows through each. Only the glass or the coating on the glass differs. The power flowing through the filaments creates the light.

The same source of illumination

God makes all of us different from one another, but by His Spirit He will bring divine illumination and power to our beings. That is something we understand. That is why we are glad we are not all alike. We can read and talk about Wesley and Moody and A.B. Simpson and Billy Sunday, about Holy Anne and Sophie the scrubwoman. It is God's planned variety and not similarity that makes beauty and interest in our world.

We should thank God for giving us our own individual personalities and temperaments and abilities. We should never waste time and energy trying to fashion ourselves after someone else, no matter how much we admire that person. God does not expect us to become identical copies of our spiritual heroes.

Actually, I have learned something very important about our efforts to become someone else. If I am tempted to copy someone whom I admire as a Christian believer, I will probably succeed only in copying his or her eccentricities and not that person's spirituality at all.

It is futile to try to assume another person's good characteristics. In only these respects should we all try to be alike: We should love God more than anything or anyone else, we should hate sin and iniquity even as Jesus hated them, and we should be willing always to obey God through the leading of His Word and His Spirit. Apart from that, it is perfectly natural for us to be ourselves, that is, different from each other.

God is the same today

I see another lesson in this Hebrews text. God has never in the past done anything good in response to faith that He is unwilling to do again. Let me turn that around and say it this way: Everything good that God has done in the past in response to faith, He is willing to do again. We need only believe and obey.

How subtle is unbelief! You read the biography of one of God's great saints and suddenly you are overcome with discouragement. You find you are comparing yourself very unfavorably with the one you have been reading about. Let me pass on some advice. Do not stop reading about God's great men and women. But keep in mind that faith and obedience, not their abilities or temperaments or dispositions, are what matter. God knows how best to use us for His glory and as His witnesses.

Faith came like a dove to the heart of Abraham — but not only to Abraham. Faith came to the rascal

Jacob as well. Faith came to Moses, it is true. But faith came also to Samson. Faith came to Sarah. Faith came as well to Rahab. I think of a simple little song we used to sing:

> Let not conscience make you linger,
> Nor of fitness fondly dream,
> All the fitness here required
> Is to feel your need of Him.

I feel good about that advice! I am not to compare myself with Abraham or Luther or Billy Graham and wonder how I can qualify as a good and useful Christian. If I truly feel my need of God, I can approach Him and expect Him to work through my uniqueness.

Be careful!

This problem of personal identity not infrequently troubles the faithful minister. The congregation has called him as their pastor and teacher, but the members have a hard time forgetting the saintly predecessor who died or who was called to another ministry. They find it hard to make room for the new minister—mainly because he is not enough like the former one. His voice is different. So are his gestures. His hair is not gray. His wife is not as friendly.

Be careful! God blesses people for their faith and obedience, not because they are old or young, bald or gray, pleasant voiced or raspy. God expects each one of us to let Him use us in helping people to a walk of spiritual blessing and victory. Not necessarily must we have had a long record as heroes in the faith to qualify.

A personal testimony

I do not look upon myself as especially notable. But I am invariably blessed when I discover God has used me to help someone else in the Christian faith. I was addressing a group of Lutherans on the life of fullness in the Holy Spirit. During a brief time of testimony after one of my messages, a young man who said he was a pastor told the group he carried in his Bible a copy of a small piece I once wrote: "The Prayer of a Minor Prophet."

I remember writing that piece. I wrote it from my heart, letting it express my own feelings about the responsibilities of a man genuinely called into the ministry of God's holy Word. In his words to the group, the young man said, "When I get discouraged, when there is trouble facing me, I open my Bible and read once more that prayer of one of God's prophets." He then expressed gratitude that in God's timing his path and mine had crossed.

Do you suppose that young man, as he read my "prayer," thought of A.W. Tozer as some kind of a hero of the faith? That would have been a very inflated idea—far beyond the assessment held by Mrs. A.W. Tozer, for instance! Most of us are inclined to quote other people, particularly those we consider to be good examples. Probably it is a good thing that we do not know them as well as their families do! Otherwise we would have to be more cautious about our quoting them and holding them up for veneration.

We can be today's people of faith

My emphasis is this: Just as those who lived in

the past had the privilege of being God's people of faith then, so do we in our own day. It is good to come to the understanding that while God wants us to be holy and Spirit-filled, He does not expect us to look like Abraham or to play the harp like David or to have the same spiritual insight given to Paul.

All of those former heroes of the faith are dead. You are alive in your generation. A Bible proverb says that it is better to be a living dog than a dead lion. You may wish to be Abraham or Isaac or Jacob, but remember that they have been asleep for long centuries, and you are still around! You can witness for your Lord today. You can still pray. You can still give of your substance to help those in need. You can still encourage the depressed.

I hope you have not missed something good from God's hand because you felt you did not measure up to Gideon or Isaiah. In this your generation, give God all of your attention! Give Him all of your love! Give Him all of your devotion and faithful service! You do not know what holy, happy secret God may want to whisper to your responsive heart.

Three simple things

Do you respond to this great possibility by asking, "How can I know?" I answer with an emphasis upon three simple things reinforced in the Word of God for those who will discern God's highest will.

First, be willing to put away known sin. Next, separate yourself from all of the attractions of the world, the flesh and the devil. Finally, offer yourself to your God and Savior in believing faith. God has never yet turned away an honest, sincere person who has come to know the eternal value of the atonement and the peace that is promised through the death and resurrection of our Lord Jesus Christ.

The only person who is incurably sick is the one who thinks he or she is well. The only person who will never be cleansed and made whole is the one who insists he or she needs no remedy. The person who comes in faith to God and confesses, "I am unclean, I am sin-sick, I am blind," will find mercy and forgiveness and life in the Lord Jesus Christ.

The doubters are still asking, "How can that be?" It can be because our Lord Jesus Christ is the Savior, the Cleanser. He is the Purifier, He is the Healer. He is the Sight-giver and the Life-giver. He alone is the Way, the Truth and the Life!

God expects us to live in faith and victory so that we may leave our Christian testimony to a new generation that undoubtedly will need it desperately. "These all died in faith," the writer to the Hebrews says. When it is our time, will we be able to meet our God knowing that we pleased Him? "Without faith it is impossible to please God."

A bright future

God is the Faithful One. We are to love Him and serve Him because He is God—not because of the gracious things He does for us or for the rewards He promises us. Our motives should be both right and genuine. But God does not expect us to forget or ignore the gracious future promises He has made to us.

It is a glorious truth that if we believe God and honor His Word, if we walk by faith in love and obedience, there will be eternal rewards for each of us in that great coming day. The rewards will differ. Wisdom and knowledge and love reside in Him who is our God. He will make the right judgments for His people.

But I for one will not be surprised if some of God's faithful people serving Him today should rise as high and shine as brightly as the heroes of faith listed in the Book of Hebrews. I say that in all truthfulness because I do not think all of the heroes of faith are dead and gone.

If we will take God at His Word, if we will believe Him and trust Him wholly in this ungodly and unfriendly world, if we will walk with Him as those men and women of faith walked in the long-ago past, God Himself will list us among His heroes of faith when the final records are opened.

7

Faith Has Eyes Only for Jesus

Is SATAN GIVING YOU A HARD TIME in your life of faith — in the Christian race you are running? Expect it if you are a believing child of God!

Satan hates your God. He hates Jesus Christ. He hates your faith. You should be aware of the devil's evil intentions. He wants you to lose the victor's crown in the race you have entered by faith through grace.

The writer of the Letter to the Hebrews gives us good New Testament counsel:

> Let us run with perseverance the race marked out for us. Let us fix our eyes on Jesus, the author and perfecter of our faith, who for the joy set before him endured the cross, scorning its shame, and sat down at the right hand of the throne of God. (Hebrews 12:1c–2)

The Holy Spirit, in giving us in the Bible a wide variety of encouragement, uses many figures to portray the believing people of God. He lets us think of ourselves as farmers, plowing and planting and reaping. He lets us think of ourselves as carpenters, planning and constructing. Again, He lets us think of ourselves as soldiers, bearing the strong armor of God and going forth to stand against the enemy.

But here, the Holy Spirit describes Christian believers as runners on the track, participants in the race of life. He provides both strong warning and loving encouragement: there is always the danger of losing the race, but there is the victor's reward awaiting those who run with patience and endurance.

There are important things each of us should know and understand about our struggles as the faithful people of God.

First, it is a fact that the Christian race is a contest. But the race is in no sense a competition between believers or between churches! As we live the life of faith, we Christians are never to be in competition with other Christians. The Bible makes this very plain. Christian churches are never told to carry on their proclamation of the Savior in a spirit of competition with other churches.

Our contest is with Satan

All of us Christians have a common enemy, that old devil, Satan. As we stand together, pray together, worship together, we repudiate him and his deceptions. He is our common foe, and he uses a variety of manipulations to hinder us in our spiritual lives.

When by faith we have entered this lifelong spiritual course, the Holy Spirit whispers, "Do you truly want to be among the victors in this discipline?" When we breathe our "Yes! Yes!" He whispers of ways that will aid us and carry us to certain victory.

The Spirit tells us to throw off everything that would hinder us in the race. He tells us to be aware of the little sins and errors that could divert us from the will of God as we run. But here is the important thing: He tells us to keep our eyes on Jesus, because He alone is our pacesetter and victorious example.

In a very real sense, faith is fixing our eyes on Jesus, keeping Jesus in full view regardless of what others may be doing all around us. This is excellent counsel, because as human beings we know we are not sufficient in ourselves. It is in our nature to look out—to look beyond ourselves for help. This world is big and deadly, and we are too weak and not wise enough to deal with it!

It is also a human trait to look beyond ourselves for assurance. We hope to find someone worthy of trust. We want someone who has made good, someone who has done what we would like to do. The Hebrews writer points us to the perfect and victorious One, our eternal High Priest, seated now at the right hand of God. He is Jesus, the Pioneer and Perfecter of our faith. He has endured the cross and is now the eternal Victor and our Advocate in heaven.

Differences of opinion

One of my not-too-secret enjoyments is having a little fun with the human translators of the Scriptures. These have been good men, I know. But as scholars and language experts, they sometimes seem confused. In the King James Version of this text, for example, Jesus is called the Author and the Finisher of our faith. Other translators have called Him the Pioneer and Perfecter. One translator simply says "the Starter and the Finisher of our faith." Scholars in another version call Jesus "the Leader and perfect Model of our faith." Still another translator suggests, "Jesus, the princely Leader and Perfecter." Yet another describes Jesus as "the Forerunner and Finisher of our faith."

Fortunately, we can put all of these suggestions together and come up with a clear, simple, forceful portrayal of Jesus. He is Jesus Christ, our Lord, the Author and the Pioneer of our faith. He is the One upon whom the Christian faith rests. He is the One who blazed the trail. He is the One who is leading us through life to a successful consummation.

In these studies from Hebrews, we have referred often to faith. The faith we are considering is not that which you might regard as your own personal faith. Jesus is more than the Author of just your faith. He is the Author, the Pioneer, the Leader, the Perfecter of the faith subscribed to by our fathers throughout the long centuries. The faith of our fathers rests on the biblical teachings and truths concerning God and the person of Jesus Christ.

It is truth that God made the heavens and the earth, that God subsists in three persons, that God spoke to men through the prophets. It is truth that God sent His one and only Son into the world in order that whoever believes in Him should not perish. It is truth that to effect our salvation, Christ had to die and to rise again. It is truth that He is now at the right hand of the Father, that He is interceding for His believing people, that He is coming back to take His people to be with Him forever. It is truth that God has promised a new heaven and a new earth, that death will finally be put down, that the enemy of our souls will be destroyed.

This, in brief outline, is the faith of our fathers. Christ Jesus is the Author and Finisher of that faith, regardless of our personal attitudes or whether or not we demonstrate perfect confidence.

But Jesus helps us with that, too! It has been my experience that if we are fully acquainted with and deeply moved by the truths on which our faith rests, our personal faith will spring up joyously in confidence and delight.

We have the perfect Model

Twenty centuries ago the Hebrew Christians were told to fix their eyes on Jesus, who for the joy set before Him had endured the cross and scorned the shame.

The physical pain and suffering Jesus endured are well known. He was beaten and scourged until His back was raw. Thorns from the mock crown pressed into His brow. Nails were driven into His hands and feet. But we should remember also the mental pain—the cruel psychological pain of shame and rejection. Jesus endured it all; He suffered it out. He scorned the shame by looking down on it as something not worthy to be mentioned when set over against the glory that was to be revealed.

Jesus' death in our stead and His resurrection from the grave are fundamental Christian doctrines on which all evangelicals agree. I can preach these truths in any Bible conference anywhere and be assured that I will be invited back.

But what *could* happen at a Bible conference would be for some fellow to whisper to another, "Tozer seems to be getting over on the legalistic side!" This could easily happen when I insist that our Lord Jesus Christ not only endured the cross and despised the shame, but *He invites us to do the same thing!*

After Jesus had rebuked Peter for saying that suffering and death could never come to the Son of Man,

> Jesus said to his disciples, "If anyone would come after me, he must deny himself and take up his cross and follow me. For whoever wants to save his life will lose it, but whoever loses his life for me will find it." (Matthew 16:24–25)

When Jesus told His disciples that the hour had come for the Son of Man to be glorified, He added:

> I tell you the truth, unless a kernel of wheat falls to the ground and dies, it remains only a single seed. But if it dies, it produces many seeds. The man who loves his life will lose it, while the man who hates his life in this world will keep it for eternal life. Whoever serves me must follow me. (John 12:24–26a)

Paul, after saying that some believers had been circumcised to avoid the persecution of Christ's cross, continued:

> May I never boast except in the cross of our Lord Jesus Christ, through which the world has been crucified to me, and I to the world. (Galatians 6:14)

To those same readers he also said:

> I have been crucified with Christ and I no longer live, but Christ lives in me. The life I live in the body, I live by faith in the Son of God, who loved me and gave himself for me. (Galatians 2:20)

How can there be any question but that our Lord Jesus Christ identified us with Himself? Instead of putting the cross on that hill outside Jerusalem, Jesus puts the cross in our lives, where it belongs!

We died with Christ

Evil-minded men hung Jesus on a wooden cross, just as Jesus had told His disciples they would. The salvation of a lost world was at stake. When He died, His body was taken down and laid in a tomb. When He arose from the dead and ascended to the right hand of God the Father, that wooden cross had no further meaning in the mind of God. None at all!

Some Christian churches are very enamored with splinters they say came from the wooden cross on which Jesus died. Apart from such dubious claims, that old wooden cross is no longer in existence. I hope we realize that when we sing "The Old Rugged Cross."

But there remains a very real cross. It is the cross you take and the cross I take as we follow our Lord Jesus who willingly took His cross. That is why I say that our Lord identifies us with Himself.

I find a deep, compelling message in the words of an old hymn no longer sung. And I am concerned for the spiritual desire now seemingly lost with the hymn:

> Oh, for that flame of living fire
>   Which shone so bright in saints of old,
> Which bade their souls to heaven aspire,
>   Calm in distress, in danger bold.
>
> Where is that Spirit, Lord, which dwelt
>   In Abram's breast and sealed him Thine,
> Which made Paul's heart with sorrow melt
>   And glow with energy divine?
>
> That Spirit which from age to age
>   Proclaimed Thy love and taught Thy ways,
> Brightened Isaiah's vivid page
>   And breathed in David's hallowed lays.

We have to ask, too, "Where is that Spirit, Lord?" Why must we cry in pathetic and plaintive manner, "Where is Thy Spirit, Lord?" I think it is because we differ from the saints of old in our relation to the cross—our attitude toward the cross.

Half right, all wrong

In our modern gospel churches, Christians have decided where to put the cross. They have made the cross objective instead of subjective. They have made the cross external instead of internal. They have made it institutional instead of experiential.

Now, the terrible thing is that they are so wrong because they are half right. They are right in making the cross objective. It was something that once stood on a hill with a man dying on it, the just for the unjust. They are right that it was an external cross—for on that cross God performed a judicial act that will last while the ages burn themselves out.

So, they are half right. But here is where they are wrong: They fail to see that there is a very real cross for you and me. There is a cross for every one of us—a cross that is subjective, internal, experiential.

Our cross is an experience within. It is a cross we voluntarily take, and it is hard, bitter, distasteful. But we take our cross for Christ's sake, and we are willing to suffer the consequences and despise the shame.

This is where people accuse Tozer of legalism, because I charge much of evangelicalism with this modern attitude: "Let the cross kill Jesus! Let Jesus do all the dying! We will live on in our faith and be happy and have fun—and we will all get to heaven in the end!"

But if we are serious about the Christian faith and the demands of our Lord Jesus Christ, we will acknowledge that the cross on the hill must become the cross in our hearts. When that cross on the hill has been transformed by the miraculous grace of the Holy Spirit into the cross in the heart, then we begin to know something of its true meaning and it will become to us the cross of power.

The world is already dead

Let me remind you of something. In Paul's word to the Galatians already referred to, Paul considers the world to be already dead. He does not plead for it. He does not try to salvage anything out of it.

Why was Paul willing to let the world go? I am sure I know the answer. Paul's love and interest and concern were for people. That is where ours should be, also. When John wrote that God so loved the world, he did not mean that God loved Hollywood or the ball park or the music hall. God did not send Jesus to give us a legitimate interest in the world's organized society. He did not send Jesus so that we could participate in the world's variety of fun and games.

God's love and concern are for people. He loves human beings made in His image, though now fallen and lost. When I say that Paul followed Christ in reckoning the world dead, I only remind you that he was turning his back on this organized and selfish world. He was not turning his back on people and their needs and their sins. Paul cared and was concerned for every individual for whom Christ died.

I should say something else here about this world and its selfish and often godless society. Why is there so much attraction to the magazines, the radio, the television, the sports, the concerts, the fun? We may be reluctant to admit it, but we have an enemy, and he has many helpers. All of these things that surely add up to fun and entertainment have an overall design of keeping people from taking God seriously. There is some great master plan that is surely succeeding in keeping men and women relatively happy in this world without ever a serious thought of God and salvation and eternal life!

Millions of men and women seem to be very content with the arrangement as it is. They do not want to be reminded at all that they are going to die and that after death comes the judgment of a holy and righteous God. They would rather remain gullible and deceived than to learn the truth about this world and the next.

God spare us from gullibility

When I was a boy on the farm, we "butchered" every year in the early fall. It was my job to coax the fattened hogs into the barn. I would throw them some corn, and they were pleased as they came grunting in with that corn still grinding in their mouths.

But in minutes they were dead. My father would then bleed them and dress them out. That is how we got our supply of pork for the winter.

The gullible pigs have never learned. Wherever they are, they are still being led to the slaughter generation after generation. All it takes is a supply of shelled corn!

You may not like the illustration, but there are plenty of gullible people who have never recognized why they are being kept so busy and so well entertained with the things that are amusing and fun. Paul said that he had caught on—and he reckoned himself dead to this world and this world dead to him.

I wonder how many of the saintly men and women who have lived for Christ throughout the centuries were accused of narrowness and legalism and of being spoilers. I think they knew and accepted the offense of the cross for what it is. I think they allowed the cross to kill their self-love, their self-confidence, their self-will, their self-pity, their self-righteousness. I think they were faithful in keeping Jesus Christ in full view, looking away from themselves and following Him all the way—even unto death.

They took the promises of God at face value. Their eyes were on the Lord and the city whose builder and maker is God. They looked beyond the passing attractions of this world to see the lovely face of Jesus Christ shining in wonderful glory.

Faith and Discipline Ready Us for Heaven

I HAVE FOUND THERE IS an entirely new way to shock complacent Christians in our churches today. These 20th century Christians go into shock when I say that it is an error to assume that being saved is to be automatically ready for heaven.

Very few people in our churches are willing to consider what the Bible actually teaches about discipline and chastening in preparing us for our heavenly home. The writer of the Letter to the Hebrews gave definite instruction to those who were children of God through faith in our Lord Jesus Christ:

> Endure hardship as discipline; God is treating you as sons. For what son is not disciplined by his father? If you are not disciplined (and everyone undergoes discipline), then you are illegitimate children and not true sons. . . . God disciplines us for our good, that we may share in his holiness. . . . Make every effort to live in peace with all men and to be holy; without holiness no one will see the Lord. (Hebrews 12:8–14)

Now, I know I will have to explain what I mean about our daily Christian lives being in preparation for an eternity in the heavenly realms. First, let us see if we are in agreement about the most important proclamation we can make concerning faith.

There is no doubt about it. First in importance concerning faith is the good news—the truth that every man and woman in our lost world may have God's gifts of forgiveness and eternal life through believing faith in Jesus Christ as Savior and Lord. It is not possible to overstate the importance of this basic truth in the Christian gospel. It has been proclaimed often. Paul gave this stark, simple instruction concerning salvation to the jailer at Philippi: "Believe in the Lord Jesus, and you will be saved—you and your household" (Acts 16:31).

As Christian believers (I am assuming you are a believer), you and I know how we have been changed and regenerated and assured of eternal life by faith in Jesus Christ and His atoning death. On the other hand, where this good news of salvation by faith is not known, religion becomes an actual bondage. If Christianity is known only as a religious institution, it may well become merely a legalistic system of religion, and the hope of eternal life becomes a delusion.

God's objective is our holiness

I have said this much about the reality and assurance of our salvation through Jesus Christ to counter the shock you may feel when I add that God wants to fully prepare you in your daily Christian life so that you will be ready indeed for heaven. Perhaps it is a good thing for you if you are shocked. It is my observation that many Christians are so cosmopolitan, so worldly-wise, so self-assured that they are past being shocked by anything!

Probably your first question as you come out of shock will be, "Have you forgotten the dying thief? Did not our Lord tell him his faith had made him ready for paradise?"

Let me share something with you. No one could love the Christian gospel and witness it to others without an understanding that the God of all grace has surely made a necessary provision for those who may trust Jesus in the final hours of life. We admit our humanness. We do not have God's wisdom and discernment. Only God is all-knowing and all-powerful. He is full of grace and truth. We can trust Him to be faithful and right in all of His dealings with us.

Remember that most believers have been found of the Lord and received His love and grace at an earlier time in their lives. Many testify to faith extending back to their childhood. Thus, they have been in God's household for a long time, and He has been trying to do something special within their beings day after day, year after year. His purpose has been to bring many sons—and daughters, too—to glory (Hebrews 1:10).

Now, if we are truly sons and daughters by faith, we will respond to the wise discipline and the necessary rebukes aimed at bringing us to the full measure of spiritual stature. God's motives are loving. Our Heavenly Father disciplines us for our own good, "that we may share in His holiness."

I have known people who seemed to be terrified

by God's loving desire that we should reflect His own holiness and goodness. As God's faithful children, we should be attracted to holiness, for holiness is God-likeness—likeness to God!

God encourages every Christian believer to follow after holiness. Holiness is to be our constant ambition—not as holy as God is holy, but holy because God is holy. We know who we are and God knows who He is. He does not ask us to be God, and He does not ask us to produce the holiness that only He Himself knows. Only God is holy absolutely; all other beings can be holy only in relative degrees.

The angels in heaven do not possess God's holiness. They are created beings and they are contented to reflect the glory of God. That is their holiness.

Holiness is not terrifying. Actually, it is amazing and wonderful that God should promise us the privilege of sharing in His nature. It is impossible for any person to be as holy as God is holy. It is encouraging that God "knows how we are formed" (Psalm 103:14). He remembers we were made of dust. So He tells us what is in His being as He thinks of us: "Be holy because I am your God and I am holy! It is My desire that you grow in grace and in the knowledge of Me. I want you to be more like Jesus, My eternal Son, every day you live!"

Our Lord endeavors to prepare us for our eternal fellowship with the saints, the martyrs, the heroes of the faith who suffered through fire and flood and blood and tears when they were God's pilgrims on this earth. Do not try to short-circuit God's plans for your discipleship and spiritual maturing here. If you and I were already prepared for heaven in that moment of our conversion, God would have taken us there instantly!

As believers and disciples, we are satisfied to know that the mysterious quality of God's holy person sets Him apart from all others and all else throughout His entire universe. God exists in Himself. His holy nature is such that we cannot comprehend Him with our minds.

God's holy nature is unique. He is of a substance not shared by any other being. Hence, God can be known only as He reveals Himself. There is absolutely no other way for us to know Him.

Today we may enjoy God's presence

In Old Testament times, whenever this utterly holy God revealed Himself in some way to humankind, terror and amazement were the reaction. People saw themselves as guilty and unclean by contrast.

Early in the Revelation, the final book of the Bible, the Apostle John describes the overwhelming nature of his encounter with the Lord of glory. He says, "When I saw him, I fell at his feet as though dead" (Revelation 1:17). John was a man, a person born into a sinful world. But he was a believer and an apostle. At the time, he was in exile "because of the word of God and the testimony of Jesus" (Revelation 1:9). But when the risen, glorified Lord Jesus appeared to him on Patmos, John sank down in abject humility and fear.

Jesus at once reassured him, stooping to place a nail-pierced hand on the prostrate apostle. "Do not be afraid," Jesus said to John. "I am the First and the Last. I am the Living One; I was dead, and behold I am alive for ever and ever! And I hold the keys of death and Hades." Then Jesus proceeded to give His apostle a writing assignment: "Write, therefore, what you have seen, what is now, and what will take place later."

I notice particularly that the Lord did not condemn John. He knew that John's weakness was the reaction to revealed divine strength. He knew that John's sense of unworthiness was the instant reaction to absolute holiness. Along with John, every redeemed human being needs the humility of spirit that can only be brought about by the manifest presence of God.

This mysterious yet gracious Presence is the air of life eternal. It is the music of existence, the poetry of the Christian life. It is the beauty and wonder of being one of Christ's own—a sinner born again, regenerated, created anew to bring glory to God. To know this Presence is the most desirable state imaginable for anyone. To live surrounded by this sense of God is not only beautiful and desirable, but it is imperative!

Know that our living Lord is unspeakably pure. He is sinless, spotless, immaculate, stainless. In His person is an absolute fullness of purity that our words can never express. This fact alone changes our entire human and moral situation and outlook. We can always be sure of the most important of all positives: God is God and God is right. He is in control. Because He is God, He will never change!

I repeat: God is right—always. That statement is the basis of all we are thinking about God.

Holiness takes time

When the eternal God Himself invites us to prepare ourselves to be with Him throughout the future ages, we can only bow in delight and gratitude, murmuring, "Oh, Lord, may Your will be
done in this poor, unworthy life!"

I can only hope that you are wise enough, desir-
ous enough and spiritual enough to face up to the
truth that every day is another day of spiritual
preparation, another day of testing and discipline
with our heavenly destination in mind. For as I
hope you have already seen, full qualification for
eternity is not instant or automatic or painless.

I hope, too, that you may begin to understand in
this context why our evangelical churches are in
such a mess. It has become popular to preach a
painless Christianity and automatic saintliness. It
has become a part of our "instant" culture. "Just
pour a little water on it, stir mildly, pick up a gospel
tract, and you are on your Christian way."

Lo, we are told, this is Bible Christianity. *It is
nothing of the sort!* To depend upon that kind of a
formula is to experience only the outer fringe, the
edge of what Christianity really is. We must be
committed to all that it means to believe in the Lord
Jesus Christ. There must be a new birth from
above; otherwise we are in religious bondage and
legalism and delusion—or worse! But when the
wonder of regeneration has taken place in our
lives, then comes the lifetime of preparation with
the guidance of the Holy Spirit.

God has told us that heaven and the glories of
the heavenly kingdom are more than humans can

ever dream or imagine. It will be neither an exhibition of the commonplace nor a democracy for the spiritually mediocre.

Why should we try to be detractors of God's gracious and rewarding plan of discipleship? God has high plans for all of His redeemed ones. It is inherent in His infinite being that His motives are love and goodness. His plans for us come out of His eternal and creative wisdom and power. Beyond that is His knowledge and regard for the astonishing potential that lies resident in human nature, long asleep in sin but awakened by the Holy Spirit in regeneration.

Yes, God is preparing us by making us disciples of Christ. A disciple is one who is in training. Being a disciple of Christ brings us to the day-by-day realities of such terms as discipline, rebuke, correction, hardship. Those are not pleasant words.

To be admonished and instructed, to be punished and reproved, to be trained and corrected— no one chooses these things because they are neither pleasant nor entertaining. But they are in God's plan for our spiritual maturity.

What will be our response?

In times of testing and hardship, I have heard Christians cry in their discouragement, "How can I believe that God loves me?" The fact is, God loves us to such a degree that He will use every necessary means to mature us until we reach "unity in the faith" and attain "to the whole measure of the fullness of Christ" (Ephesians 4:13).

A critic may cringe and charge that God is breaking our spirits, that we will be worth nothing as a result, that we will wear only a sad, hang-dog look for eternity. Oh, no! That is not true. What God plans is to bring us into accord with the wisdom and power and holiness that flow eternally from His throne.

God's loving motive is to bring us into total harmony with Himself so that moral power and holy usefulness become ours in this world and in the world to come.

This has been a message from my heart about down-to-earth preparation that will result in readiness for heaven's joys. Let me therefore conclude with a simple, down-to-earth illustration—the example of a newborn baby brought suddenly into the confusion of our noisy world.

Is the little fellow "ready" for this world in which he must live? When the time of his birth neared, the doctor told the parents-to-be, "The baby is ready!" So, as the baby was born, it could have been said in the biological sense that he was "ready."

But what do you really think? You must know that the baby is not really ready at all! From the first little whack he gets to make him cry and get his breath right on for the next 18 or 20 years, that baby and child and young man will need to learn much about his environment. He will need to mature day by day.

In the broader social and human sense, he is not ready for this world until years have passed and he has completed his formal education. So it is with the Christian believer who has confessed his or her faith in Jesus Christ. Oh, yes, he or she is forgiven and "saved." But is he, is she automatically prepared for heaven and all of the eternal glories above?

To say yes is to be ridiculous. You might as well say that you can pick up a newborn baby, prop him up in the chair of the nation's president or prime minister, and whisper in his ear that he is ready to govern.

My mind returns frequently to some of the old Christian saints who often prayed in their faith, "O God, we know this world is only a dressing room for the heaven to come!" They were very close to the truth in their vision of what God has planned for His children.

In summary: Down here the orchestra merely rehearses; over there we will give the concert. Here, we ready our garments of righteousness; over there we will wear them at the wedding of the Lamb.

Faith Is Not Given Us to Fail

COMING INTO THE CHRISTIAN LIFE by faith does
not release us from the cautions God has given
us in His Word. Study the Bible seriously, and you
will find that God desires His church to be watchful
and alert, diligent in the humble life of faith and
trust.

In the Letter to the Hebrews, we come to a sober-
ing caution and a spiritual responsibility:

> See to it that no one misses the grace of God
> and that no bitter root grows up to cause trou-
> ble and defile many. (Hebrews 12:15)

In the King James Version, this verse carries an
even stronger warning: "Looking diligently lest any
man fail of the grace of God . . ."

We know our human natures, and we do not
deny our human weaknesses. We confess that we
need both the cautions and the encouragements
God has provided. We know very well our need to
lean on the divine promises for the better kind of
life—the life of faith and trust that is pleasing to
God.

This Letter to the Hebrews was written in the first

place to provide caution and encouragement. And it still speaks plainly to us today. Its message and appeal come to us with urgency: "There are decisions to be made. You must dare to believe! You must dare to obey God! Go on over to the victory side where there is forgiveness and blessing from the eternal Son, who is now your great High Priest in the heavenlies!"

The cautions may be negative, but our Lord's emphasis is positive: "Each of you must press forward in your Christian faith and experience! Be diligent and be wise, and you will not be among those who delay and question and hold back!"

Now, what warning was the writer trying to give us when he said that some people might miss the grace of God—might fail of the grace of God? And what warning should we take from the writer's reference to some who would actually fall away?

> It is impossible for those who have once been enlightened, who have tasted the heavenly gift, who have shared in the Holy Spirit, who have tasted the goodness of the word of God and the powers of the coming age, if they fall away, to be brought back to repentance, because to their loss they are crucifying the Son of God all over again and subjecting him to public disgrace. (Hebrews 6:4–6)

Controversial statements

The interpretation of these statements has always produced differences of opinion among Christians. My purpose is not to engage in argument. Rather, I am hopeful that some of these considerations I am proposing will be helpful if you feel concerned or even confused.

Ministers have said to me that there are so many positive Scriptures that they just work around the more difficult and controversial sections. When I preach month after month in a specific book of the Bible, I try faithfully to deal with the "hard-to-understand" passages when I come to them.

For centuries, there have been differences in the interpretation of certain verses relating to the faith and endurance of Christian believers—the "perseverance of the saints," as some call it. In Christian theology, so the dictionaries say, this simply means "the continuance in a state of grace until it is succeeded by a state of glory."

I look back into church history, and in my own mind, I can visualize John Calvin and John Arminius—who polarized the issue of God's sovereignty versus man's free will—squaring off in their own differences at this point. But why should this be made such a great test in the area of our Christian fellowship?

People have cornered me and pressured me, asking pointedly, "Are you Calvinistic or Arminian in doctrine?" I think I have effectively parried this thrust by repeating a conversation I once had with a prominent English clergyman of our times. He spoke to me of another minister of his acquaintance, and I asked, "He is a Calvinist, I presume?"

My minister friend smiled with good humor. "Well," he replied, "I think he is what we might call an equivocating Calvinist!" From a personal point of view and to answer the curious, I would say that the phrase also describes me fairly well!

We need to disagree graciously

I have always said that these are personal matters for each of us to determine in our own sincere lives of faith. I have found many thoughtful people in our fellowship who do not want to be pushed from a position of charity and understanding to the extreme edge of any doctrines, particularly where the deity and the uniqueness of Jesus Christ are not in question.

Scores of books have been written by people who have taken opposite sides on some of these difficult passages of Scripture. I have read and studied many of these books.

In this context, I recall a friend's story. He told me that he had discovered a woodworking shop where all varieties of wooden products, like clothes pins and chair legs, were made and sold. There was a rather startling sign in front of the shop. It read: "All Kinds of Twisting and Turning Done Here." When I have read the narrow, partisan arguments set forth in some of these books I mention, I have felt they too could use the words as an overall title: *All Kinds of Twisting and Turning Done Here*!

We do well to remember that we are Christ's only representatives in an evil world and in a very self-centered society. I believe our Lord wants us to be day-by-day examples in the gracious art of putting our Christian love and concern ahead of any divisive dialogue.

One school of thought has always insisted that those who have fallen away could not have been genuine believers. They may have had the appearance of being Christians, but they were not. They could speak the language of Christians. They had the reputation of being Christian believers. They may have won the trust and confidence of the Christians around them, but they had not attained unto the grace of God. And because they had missed, in some way or another, the grace of God, they had fallen away.

On the other side, there are many reasons for considering those who have fallen away as once Christian believers. They were described as enlightened, as having shared in the Holy Spirit, as having tasted the goodness of the Word of God and the powers of the coming age.

But, the arguers persist, they merely had received light. They had only tasted. They may have *recognized* the Holy Spirit, but they did not possess Him. As a result they fell away.

We should compare Scripture with Scripture

When it comes to the original Greek, I do not profess to be a scholar. But I do know how to compare the basic meaning of the same words when they are used in different places in the Scriptures. Some teachers have commented: "Enlightened—that means they merely had light, but they were not born again. They merely received light."

But when Paul wrote to remind the Ephesian Christians of his prayer that the eyes of their understanding would be enlightened, he used the very same word we find in Hebrews 6:4. Paul was praying for an advanced spiritual state for genuine Christians whom he called saints and chosen of God. Clearly *enlightened* may mean much more than merely receiving information about the gospel.

The next expression refers to their tasting of the heavenly gift, the goodness of the Word of God and the powers of the coming age. The word *tasted* has caused some to conclude that these to whom the writer refers merely licked at it—sampled it—to see if they liked it, and decided that they did not. But the very word used for tasting here is also used in Hebrews 2:9, where we are told that Christ "tasted death for everyone." If tasting the heavenly gift means merely nibbling but never swallowing and digesting, are we to say the same for Christ, who tasted death for everyone? Christ *experienced* death. We can hardly conclude other than that the people mentioned in Hebrews 6 likewise had experienced the heavenly gift, the goodness of the Word of God and the powers of the coming age.

Then there is the expression, "who have shared in the Holy Spirit." Those who suppose these were not genuine Christians minimize this sharing in the Holy Spirit. "They went along with Him, but they never really possessed Him."

But I find this same Greek word translated "sharing" or "partaking of" used elsewhere in the Scriptures for accepting, receiving, eating. I have to believe this word means actual experience, also. These had received and experienced the Holy Spirit.

This would indicate that those who had experienced and actually shared in spiritual attainments could fall away, some even "crucifying the Son of God all over again" to the point they could not be brought back to repentance.

Backsliding and the "unpardonable sin"

Right here, I would like to suggest a point for clarification. I do not think we are referring to what we commonly call "backsliding" when we are considering what it may mean to fall away. Look at Peter. He failed miserably, but he was forgiven and became a great apostle. Look at Mark. He went back for a time, but he was restored and served Christ until he died.

We also know that there have been many backslidden Christians who have agonized over the possibility of having committed the unpardonable sin. I have discovered a very helpful rule in this matter. I believe it holds good throughout the whole church of God around the world. *Anyone who is concerned about having committed the unpardonable sin may be sure he or she has not!*

Any person who has ever committed that dark and dread unpardonable sin feels no guilt and confesses no worry. Jesus dealt with the Pharisees and told them face to face that their expressions concerning His person and their attributing the work of the Holy Spirit to the devil were evidences of the unpardonable sin. But His warning caused them no worry. They still believed themselves to be entirely righteous! They felt no need for repentance, no sorrow for sin, no guilt for unbelief. "Do not worry about us," was their attitude. "We do not have any problem!"

Returning to our rule for Christians with guilt and concern, the very fact that a person is worried and concerned indicates that the Spirit of God is still working in his or her life.

Being human and therefore finite, we may not know in this life all that the inspired writer meant when he used the words *fall away*. I suggest that to actually fall away means that the person has no worry about his or her spiritual defection. He or she shrugs it all off as though it was a foolish relationship in the first place.

Concerning the words, "it is impossible . . . to be brought back to repentance," I have found a helpful suggestion. Let me refer to the example of a sinning man in the church at Corinth:

> It is actually reported that there is sexual immorality among you, and of a kind that does not occur even among pagans: A man has his father's wife. And you are proud! Shouldn't you rather have been filled with grief and have put out of your fellowship the man who did this? Even though I am not physically present, I am with you in spirit. And I have already passed judgment on the one who did this, just as if I were present. When you are assembled in the name of our Lord Jesus and I am with you in spirit, and the power of our Lord Jesus is present, hand this man over to Satan, so that the sinful nature may be destroyed and his spirit saved on the day of the Lord. (1 Corinthians 5:1–5)

With God all things are possible

It is plain that Paul condemned this man for his incestuous acts, and it appears further that he could not be brought to repentance by the Corinthian church. So Paul said, "We will hand him over to Satan for the destruction of the flesh that the spirit may be saved in the coming day of our Lord Jesus Christ."

In the light of this action and the instructions of Paul given to the believers in the church, I ask you a question—and I think it is a searching question: May we not conclude in faith, relative to those the church cannot bring to repentance, that God Himself may accomplish it, even by bringing them to the point of death and turning them around to Himself? The suggestion is surely inherent in this study of the incestuous man, for we learn in Second Corinthians that he indeed repented.

Some of these questions have been on the lips of Christians throughout the centuries. Some of them have been bitterly argued. There are believers still who spend much time and effort trying to convert other people to their opinions concerning them.

When it comes to this issue of the impossibility of renewing a person to repentance, the question has long ago been settled in my own heart and mind: *I am not going back!*

For me, the question of falling away is only academic. It is academic and not real to all Christian believers who, like their Savior, have set their faces like a flint. We will follow the Lamb wherever He leads us!

We have not come into the Christian faith to promote or protect shallow Christian experience. Neither is it our calling to defend the coldness of heart that is all too apparent in Christian circles. Let us never, never defend such coldness of heart! Rather, let us covenant to follow Jesus Christ fully and faithfully. We know that He will faithfully and lovingly do His part to keep us and sustain us.

God's first-aid kit

But, you ask, "What if I fail? What if I stumble through some weakness of the flesh?" Probably the very best way for me to close out this discussion is to remind you of God's first-aid kit for His devoted family.

I had some part in raising a family of six boys and one girl. As a family, we could never have made it without the first-aid kit. There was hardly a time during those years that we were not giving attention to a cut or a bruise, a cold or an illness. It is remarkable that they all survived—and in good health!

God has provided an effective truth—I call it our spiritual first-aid kit—in John's first letter:

> If we claim to be without sin, we deceive ourselves and the truth is not in us. If we confess our sins, he is faithful and just and will forgive us our sins and purify us from all unrighteousness. If we claim we have not sinned, we make him out to be a liar and his word has no place in our lives.
>
> My dear children, I write this to you so that you will not sin. But if anybody does sin, we have one who speaks to the Father in our defense—Jesus Christ, the Righteous One. He is the atoning sacrifice for our sins, and not only for ours but also for the sins of the whole world. (1 John 1:8–2:2)

That is a plain, blunt, helpful message from the

Scriptures. If you say you have not sinned, you are lying! Jesus is our great High Priest, and He appears with the Father on our behalf. He is our Advocate, our Intercessor. Go to Him, confess your sin and your need, and He will cleanse and forgive. He will bless and heal.

No turning back!

Now, we have come through these difficult, hard-to-understand passages, and it remains for us to determine that we are committed followers of the Lamb. We are not going back! I never want to experience whatever it means to fall away, to fail the God who is full of grace and truth. I do not want to know—or experience—whatever it means to fall away.

I do not want to know any more about hell. What I do know about hell is enough to make me want to know much more about heaven and our Savior, who is already there.

I do not want to find out how far I can go toward the edge without finally perishing. But I do want to know, by the grace of God, how closely and carefully I can walk with Him in faith and blessing and victory.

Faith's Manifesto: We Claim God *Now*!

How MANY ARE WITHIN THE ranks of the Christian church by confession of faith—yet living daily as spiritual paupers and beggars, as though Christ Jesus had never been raised from the dead?

I long for every believer in the church of our Lord to join me in a clear-cut manifesto to our times. I want it to be a declaration of our intentions to restore Christ to the place that is rightfully His in our personal lives, in our family situations and in the fellowship of the churches that bear His name.

Too many within the Christian church seem able to do no better than to be concerned—and then to be apologetic. Let me say that the time for apologies is long past! The need today is for men and women of faith and courage and daring. The need is for Christians who are so concerned for the presence of Jesus Christ in their midst that they will demonstrate the standards of godliness and biblical holiness as a rebuke to this wicked and perverse generation.

The church, generally speaking, is afflicted with a dread, lingering illness that shows itself daily in the apathy and spiritual paralysis of its members.

How can it be otherwise when 20th-century Christians refuse to acknowledge the sharp moral antithesis that God Himself has set between the church, as the body of Christ, and this present world with its own human systems?

The differences between the churchly world and the followers of the Lamb are so basic that they can never be reconciled and they can never be negotiated. God never promised His believing people that they would become a popular majority in this earthly scene. But the inspired writer to the suffering Hebrew Christians in the first century promised something better. He emphasized the availability of Jesus, our Lord and Savior, in the life of the true Body, His church:

> You have not come to a mountain that can be touched and that is burning with fire. . . . But you have come to Mount Zion, to the heavenly Jerusalem, the city of the living God. . . . You have come to God, the judge of all men, to the spirits of righteous men made perfect, to Jesus the mediator of a new covenant, and to the sprinkled blood that speaks a better word than the blood of Abel. (Hebrews 12:18, 22–25)

The blessings are here and now

These warm, glowing New Testament words speak of God's great plan for Christ's life to be exhibited constantly in the faithful and believing church. They speak of great treasures and glorious realities that we should presently be enjoying in our Christian life and walk.

The Hebrews writer says plainly that if we are a

New Testament church, we have come to the joys of Mount Zion and to the city of the living God, the heavenly Jerusalem. He says we are surrounded by an innumerable company of angels. He reminds us, without any hesitation, that by our faith we are already included in the general assembly and church of the Firstborn. He states that our names are written in heaven. He does not hold back: he tells us that we are perfectly related to the Judge of all and to the spirits of just men made perfect!

Because there are no limitations known to our God, the writer presses on to assure us of the reality of our fellowship with Jesus, the mediator of the new covenant, and of His blood, which speaks better things than the blood of Abel that cried out for revenge.

These are all reasons why we should take our stand, put ourselves on record. This revelation of what God expects of the New Testament church makes me fall down before the Lord. I find myself crying in faith and determination: "Jesus, I will trust You and follow You in this present evil age. I will trust You to be my very life and sufficiency in the fellowship and joy of the body of believers, Your church!"

Repeat: this is a *present* reality

Let me hasten to the Spirit's emphasis here to Christian believers. The inspired Word of God insists that the reality and the blessings from the heart of the living Christ are not reserved for some future and heavenly age.

We are forced to part company with a great segment of popular Christian theology which congenially offers us soothing advice: "Let's not get mixed up or sidetracked. All of these precious things are references to heaven. So we will just bide our time, and we will have it all—some day!" Actually, there is no mention at all of a future heaven in these promises to the church. There is no reference to the day we will die. Rather, the New Testament church of Jesus Christ is to know and possess these realities now.

We can meet God and His Spirit in blessed reality now! We can know and commune with our Lord Jesus Christ in our heart of hearts now! We may know the joy of sensing all around us God's innumerable company and the fellowship with the church of the Firstborn *now*!

As committed Christians, we know what we believe and we know what God has done for us. We want to make it plain to our own day and age that we are highly privileged to be part of a Christian church in God's plan and in God's will. We are thankful for the dimensions of His grace and love. We know where we stand in faith, and we are not bound by ecclesiastical traditions, except where we choose to be and intelligently and openly desire to be.

Because we experience the life of Jesus Christ in the body, we need not be engaged in finding out what other religious groups are doing. Our statement of faith is clear: through the Holy Spirit we get our instructions from the throne of God as we study and lean upon His revelation in the Scriptures.

We desire to make it very plain that we have a valid reason for our assemblies and fellowship. It is a reason of spiritual life and spiritual maturity. It is not a social reason—even though our Christian fellowship does have social implications.

The negatives must be dealt with

Let me remind you that the writer to the Hebrew Christians began this section with a negative reference: "You have not come to [Sinai]," and then he proceeds to the positive declaration, "You have come to Mount Zion." It is fitting that we consider the negative before dealing with the positive. How can anyone deny that a portion of our Christian teaching has always taken into account the negative concerns? When we stand up for Jesus, it means that there are some things that we will be against.

This is the way it is in this world. We do not deny it, and we do not apologize for it. To say that we will never discuss anything in the negative would be similar to saying that there is only one side of a coin. If I should try to split all of my Canadian quarters right through the middle because I am impressed with the likeness of the Queen but I want to get rid of the likeness of the elk on the other side, someone might soon appear at 5 Old Orchard Road to deal with me. "A nice old man," they would comment condescendingly, "but he has slipped his trolley."

There is polarity in the universe, and we do well to recognize it. In order for right to be established and grow, wrong must be exterminated, or at least minimized. Of these words, *exterminate* and *minimize*, I prefer *exterminate*. I like to see the extinction of things that are wrong and unworthy.

We are always going to have to deal with the negatives—the things that are offensive and out of place—in order that we may emphasize the things that are right and that have a rightful place.

I am reminded that when Jesus came to offer Himself to Israel, there was much that He was forced to oppose. Much of His teaching was against the negatives in the religious professions of the Pharisees. He found it necessary to expose the negative concepts they held and to oppose their distorted and unworthy views of God's love and mercy. It is surely just a pipedream to imagine that a man with a head full of error and a heart full of heresy can receive truth into his mind and being.

When Martin Luther came into his effective ministry, he had to personally engage the power of Rome, and he dared to stand against it. The plain-speaking evangelist, Charles Finney, had to meet and defeat the dead Christian orthodoxy of his day in order to release the power of God's Word for the salvation of men and women.

The Christians of our own day who still think they can be "carried to the skies on flow'ry beds of ease" are wrong, terribly wrong! We must face up to what is going on in the churches and meet it as men and women of God. It is not enough just to show a smiling countenance and insist that we are hoping for the best. Where we see there is wrong, we must face up to it, show why it is wrong and dismiss it; and then plant truth in its place. A builder dares not erect any structure until he has cleared the sand and debris away in order to place the foundation squarely down on rock.

Some things we must oppose

As Christian believers, we must stand together against some things. So, if you hear anyone saying that A.W. Tozer preaches a good deal that is negative, just smile and agree. "That is because he preaches the Bible!"

Here are some of the things we oppose:

We are against the many modern idols that have been allowed to creep into the churches. We are against the "unauthorized fire" that is being offered on the altars of the Lord. We are against the modern gods that are being adopted in our sanctuaries. We are specifically against the baptized foolery and sanctified frivolity that have come to the fore, even in conservative Christian churches.

We hold firmly to our belief that the Christian church is a divinely appointed body and that as a church we are called to worship and witness for Christ. We believe in another dimension also: that we are called to an attitude of separation from the things of this world that grieve the heart of God.

We are against this world's ways and its false values. We are against this world's follies and its vain pleasures. We are against this world's greed and sinful ambitions. We are against this world's vices and its carnal habits.

We believe this spells out clearly the Bible truth of separation. God asks us to stand boldly against anything or anyone who hurts or hinders this New Testament body of Christians. We dare to state that an apathetic tolerance is not necessarily a virtue. It may be a downright vice if it is given to excusing hurtful abuses.

Actually, the body of Christ has been given deposits of love and faith that bring self-healing and self-building. But if the church tolerates within itself those things that harm and destroy, it will not heal itself—it will wither! Therefore, it is necessary for us to stand with and teach the Bible and all its truths. The Word of God is the "antibiotic" that seeks out and destroys the viruses that would plague the life of the church.

Now, to the positive side!

But there is a positive side. We do need to rejoice in the positive blessings that come to us through Jesus Christ our Lord. His positive will is our glory!

It is a positive reality that we do not have to wait for that day when Christ is fully revealed to know the everlasting joys and possess the everlasting treasures that have come to us through His death, resurrection and glorification.

The Apostle Paul does not advise us to wait until we get to heaven. In his Letter to the Ephesians, he encourages us to claim our spiritual inheritance and heavenly blessings now:

> Praise be to the God and Father of our Lord Jesus Christ, who has blessed us in the heavenly realms with every spiritual blessing in Christ. . . . He predestined us to be adopted as his sons through Jesus Christ [that is here and now] . . . to the praise of his glorious grace, which he has freely given us in the One he loves [that is also here and now]. . . . In him we have redemption through his blood, the forgiveness of sins, in accordance with the riches

of God's grace [that, too, is now]. . . . And he made known to us the mystery of his will according to his good pleasure, which he purposed in Christ. . . . (Ephesians 1:3–9)

Paul then races on into the future to show us that all of our gracious blessings which we now have in Christ constitute only the prelude for all of the ages to come. It is a remarkable listing of the shining glories to which we, as members of the body of Christ, are called in our pilgrimage here.

Note that I am speaking of the *body of Christ*, not what is frequently referred to as the institutional Christian church. It can be fairly said that the institutional church is largely known in the world as an organization and not as a living organism. The institutional church offers many good things to its members, but it does not necessarily recognize the true glory of Christ's life within. It lives and thrives on sociability, amusements, group activities — things that may be innocent and pleasant and nice but which lack the glories of the church of the living God.

That wondrous delight which the disciples felt when they met with their risen Lord is not there. There is no delight, no adoration, no worship except what is superimposed by the beauty of the stained glass windows and the solemnity of organ tones.

It is paramount that the church of Jesus Christ should be concerned for the supreme gifts of God. The church should be concerned for those spiritual blessings that have been bought by the blood of Jesus Christ and made accessible to us now through the ministries of the eternal Spirit of God.

But we are citizens of heaven

The church of Jesus Christ, His believing body on earth, recognizes that "our citizenship is in heaven. And we eagerly await a Savior from there, the Lord Jesus Christ" (Philippians 3:20). The believing Christian agrees that he or she is a migrant and a pilgrim.

To these believers, God has imparted His own nature. They have a distinct sense of belonging to one another while they live—almost as exiles—in an unfriendly world. These earthly citizens of heaven speak a common language—that of their constitution, which is the Bible, the Word of God. They love to sing the songs of Zion, for they are loyal to the same Lord and King. Thus the Christians come together where the life of the assembly is the life of Christ.

This is the Bible pattern. God the Father is there. Christ the Son is present. The Holy Spirit indwells each member. The life and spirit of Christ is the true glory of the church.

Let us not overlook the fact that the "inner man" is a real being as certainly as the eternal, physical "man" is a real being. For certain the soul within us has ears and can hear the voice of God. The spirit within us can experience and taste the glories of God in a blessed fellowship now. Such is the joyful purpose of the church!

I dare to remind you, as a fellow-believer, that God has set before us a rich table of blessings. He is saying, "This is all yours, and it is for you now!" God tells us that we share in fellowship with all of those who are enjoying His blessings in the heavenlies. He is saying, "Share these blessings! They are all yours. And Christ, your elder Brother, is in the midst, presiding over My table!"

The reality of our spiritual blessings in Christ can never be apprehended by a downright secular philosophy. The deaf person will never acknowledge the satisfying impact of a symphony orchestra. He or she cannot hear. The ailing man on a starvation diet cannot describe the taste and delight of good, nutritional food. He is on his death course.

So, the person who is dead in trespasses and sins but brags of culture and education and refinement can only shrug and walk away when we try to describe the glory of God, the beauty of Jesus, the wonder of the Holy Spirit and the present accessibility of Zion, city of God.

But when that person shrugs and walks away, we still have our smile and our joy. We know what we have found: the "spirits of righteous men made perfect."

Are we falling short of the goal?

Are we so absorbed with worldly affairs that we do not enjoy God's promised blessings as we should—right now? Why are we not trusting God to let us inspire one another as we sense the presence of these good, invisible gifts? They are the things that are ours in Christ now because we are part of the body of Christ. Oh, for the spiritual insight and godly trust of an Elisha!

Remember that Elisha, the prophet in a day long past, lived so close to God that he was able to tell

Israel what their great foe, Aram, was doing. The king of Aram inquired of his forces if there was a spy in the ranks. His own people gave him this answer: "Elisha, the prophet who is in Israel, tells the king of Israel the very words you speak in your bedroom" (2 Kings 6:12). So the king "sent horses and chariots and a strong force" to surround Dothan, Elisha's city.

The next morning, Elisha's young assistant came rushing in, pale-faced and trembling, to report the military build-up. "Oh, my lord, what shall we do?" he cried. But the old prophet just bowed his shaggy head in reverent prayer: "Lord, open his eyes so he may see."

And God answered the prophet's prayer. God opened the young man's eyes and let him see the true situation. God showed him the presence of the heavenly host between the city and the enemy forces. The young man "saw the hills full of horses and chariots of fire all around Elisha."

As the enemy troops advanced, Elisha prayed again. "Strike these people with blindness." God did so, and Elisha himself led the confused and blinded troops to Samaria and to Israel's king.

The story ends as well as any in the whole Old Testament. When the king asked Elisha if he should kill the Aramean prisoners, Elisha intervened. "Do not kill them. Set food and water before them so that they may eat and drink and then go back to their master." And that is just what they did. The Bible record concludes with great significance: "So the bands from Aram stopped raiding Israel's territory" (6:23).

Our conclusion

Here, then, is the conclusion of our manifesto of faith:

If those who call themselves the people of God would give up their carnality and worldly-mindedness, if they would live with the reality that Jesus is victor at the heavenly controls, they could be the kind of New Testament church that makes glad the heart of God. There would be such an overflow of the Holy Spirit's gifts and graces that their spirituality would be effective in every contact and activity, just as it was in New Testament times.

God grant that it may be so!

Faith Will Endure the Final Shaking

THE LIVING GOD DOES NOT ASK US to believe Him and honor Him only because of His mighty acts done in the past. The writer to the Hebrews informs us of a spectacular future judgment promised by God. It will be a "shaking" of His creation and the actual removal of temporal things to ensure that "what cannot be shaken may remain."

This is the brief review of God's acts provided in the Letter to the Hebrews:

> See to it that you do not refuse him who speaks. If they did not escape when they refused him who warned them on earth, how much less will we, if we turn away from him who warns from heaven? At that time his voice shook the earth, but now he has promised, "Once more I will shake not only the earth but also the heavens." The words "once more" indicate the removing of what can be shaken—that is, created things—so that what cannot be shaken may remain.
>
> Therefore, since we are receiving a kingdom that cannot be shaken, let us be thankful, and

so worship God acceptably with reverence and awe, for our "God is a consuming fire." (Hebrews 12:25–29)

We believe the Holy Spirit of God is the true Author of what is written here. We note the warning that men and women may be guilty of refusing to heed the God who speaks to His creation on earth.

God's first divine act described in these verses was His giving of the Law—the Ten Commandments. On Mount Sinai He spoke to Moses and through him to the people of Israel. The second reference is to the gospel—God's revealing from heaven His grace, mercy and love in the person of Jesus Christ, the eternal Son.

When this message was written to the early church nearly 2,000 years ago, both of these mighty, divine acts were already history. God had spoken to the fallen human race, first from the mount, from the earth, and then from heaven itself with the plan of redemption through Jesus Christ.

But the Hebrews text continues with the promise of a future act of God. It speaks of the great day of consummation—the final judgment that is often mentioned in the Scriptures.

God's word at Sinai

First, I want to review the two great acts of God in the past. The Old Testament record makes it clear that God chose the nation of Israel to witness and exemplify Him before a lost, sinful humanity. From that nation as well would come the promised Messiah and Savior.

The Israelites, at the time God spoke from Sinai, had just been delivered from grinding slavery and oppression in Egypt. For four centuries they had been surrounded and influenced by Egyptian paganism. Three months after leaving Egypt en route to Canaan, Israel under Moses' leadership had come to the rugged wilderness terrain of Sinai. The dark red granite peaks clustered ahead of them, rising to heights of 8,000 feet.

Israel was encamped in an area of open ground that looked upward to the peak of Mount Sinai. Dangers and uncertainties loomed ahead of them. Surely these chosen children of Israel did not realize that they were about to participate in an awesome, even terrifying encounter with the Lord, their God. It was to be an event unprecedented in human history. The living God was ready to declare His holy, moral will to a young nation. Israel's intended role was to communicate that will to an earthly society in a sin-cursed world.

God called Moses to go up into the mountain. He told him to prepare the people of Israel to receive His sacred Law. On Sinai, God in a mighty, significant act spoke from the earthly mountain, declaring His moral will for His people.

The giving of the Law on Sinai was accompanied by supernatural terror, according to the Scriptures. The mountain burned with fire. There was darkness and tempest. There were the sounds of a mighty trumpet and the divine Voice, so overpowering that the encamped people pleaded that they could not endure it and begged that they should not have to hear it.

The experience was so far beyond the limits of

normal human expression that Moses cried, "I am trembling with fear!" God was dramatizing the necessity for people to live according to His will. In unforgettable fashion, God was setting before human beings the high principles of morality that He requires of His creatures. *YES, BUT HOW? WITHOUT BEING LEGALSTIC?*

God said, "This is what I expect"

It was in those Ten Commandments that God said to His earthly people, "Here is what I expect from you, My covenant people. My Law declares specifically your individual moral duty to Me and to your fellow beings." God promised Israel through Moses: "If you obey me fully and keep my covenant, . . . you will be for me a kingdom of priests and a holy nation" (Exodus 19:5–6). For the first time in history, men and women could actually be measured in the performance of their moral duties both to God and to their fellow beings. *WORK? OR LEGAL MERIT*

History tells us how thoroughly Israel disregarded God's Word. That was Israel's great tragedy: she disregarded the word from God.

God bore patiently with His erring people. He brought them into the promised land of Canaan. He made them a great nation—under David and Solomon, dominant over all the surrounding nations. Israel's temple atop Mount Moriah was a thing of beauty and splendor.

History tells us that Israel lost her temple. The nation lost her king. The people were driven from their land and scattered among the nations. Ultimately a remnant returned to struggle against superpowers that controlled their homeland. In the fullness of time God sent Messiah. Israel failed to recognize Him. Instead, she put Him to death on a cross. Short decades later, Rome mercilessly devastated Jerusalem and blotted Israel from national existence. In all the succeeding centuries, the Jews have known trouble and persecution. They have wandered the earth. The famed wailing wall in present-day Jerusalem is a continuing symbol of Israel's great tragedy: her failure to hear and heed the God who spoke so eloquently on earth from Sinai. *AND OLIVET (MATH 5)*

I will only remind you, for you surely know it well, that many people have declared the Ten Commandments no longer valid, no longer relevant in our society. I watch the papers to check on the sermon topics of my fellow ministers, and it is apparent that Christian churches are not paying attention to the Ten Commandments.

Dwight L. Moody preached often on the Commandments. John Wesley said he preached the commands of the Law in order to prepare the way for the gospel. R.A. Torrey told ministers if they did not preach the Law they would have no response to the preaching of the gospel. It is the Law that prepares us for the gospel. It is the Law that shows us our need for the gospel of salvation and forgiveness. *I TOTALLY AGREE, I LOVE GOD'S LAW BUT WHAT ABOUT THE ONE WHO GAVE "LEGALISM"!*

That Law has not been annulled

When I said the Ten Commandments are no longer in vogue, I referred to common attitudes held generally among unbelievers. In our Christian churches, we generally respond, "Well, we are not living under the Law; we are living under God's grace!"

It is accurate to say that our binding obligation is not to Old Testament Law. As believing Christians, we are under Christ's higher law—that which is represented in His love and grace. It is true that if we are in Christ, His better law of love is operative in our lives.

Is that a big relief to us? Something else needs to be said about God's Law and God's will and God's grace. Everything that is morally commanded in the Ten Commandments still comprises the moral principles that are the will of God for His people. As believing, regenerated Christians, we must acknowledge that God's moral will for His people—then and now—has not changed.

God expressed His will for His covenant people. He said, for example, "You shall have no other gods. . . . You shall not make for yourself an idol. . . . You shall not bow down to them or worship them" (Exodus 20:3–5). It has always been God's will that His people shun idolatry.

We take our position in God's grace that we are not bound by Mosaic Law. Are we free, then, to worship idols? No, of course not! We are in our Savior, Jesus Christ, by faith. We have met God. We love Him with our whole being. We admire Him and we worship Him. To us, it would be utterly senseless to worship an idol made by the hands of human beings. That is our higher reason—and it confirms the moral will of God.

We can apply the same moral and spiritual standards of our faith to the matters of taking the name of the Lord in vain, to covetousness and murder and adultery and stealing and lying. We are not bound by the exterior chains of the old Law—true. If we are what Christ means us to be through love and grace, that kind of external allegiance is not necessary.

The Apostle Paul expressed well for us this new principle of grace:

> Through Christ Jesus the law of the Spirit of life set me free from the law of sin and death. For what the law was powerless to do in that it was weakened by the sinful nature, God did by sending his own Son in the likeness of sinful man to be a sin offering. And so he condemned sin in sinful man, in order that the righteous requirements of the law might be fully met in us, who do not live according to the sinful nature but according to the Spirit. (Romans 8:2–4)

God's second mighty act

Now, let us review the second mighty act of God—the giving of this gospel of grace. The gospel of our Lord Jesus Christ is the declaration of God's redemptive will for men and women on this earth.

Quite surely we can agree that this act was more completely divine than the first. I say so because of the participation of the three Persons of the Godhead—Father, Son and Holy Spirit—in the plan of salvation for the lost.

This brings us to the mystery and miracle of the Incarnation—God coming to take our humanity and our flesh, yet without sin. Luke quotes the message of the angel Gabriel to Mary:

> You have found favor with God. You will be with child and give birth to a son, and you are

> to give him the name Jesus. He will be great
> and will be called the Son of the Most High.
> . . . The Holy Spirit will come upon you, and
> the power of the Most High will overshadow
> you. So the holy one to be born will be called
> the Son of God." (Luke 1:30–35)

The overshadowing of the Most High, the Father; the energy of the Holy Spirit; the enfleshment of the eternal Son—here were the Persons of the Godhead cooperating in a gracious act on behalf of lost men and women.

Later, at the crucifixion, in that most important of all moments for a lost, death-doomed race, the three Persons of the Godhead are again in full view. Our writer to the Hebrews expressed it concisely: "Christ . . . through the eternal Spirit offered himself unblemished to God" (9:14).

Then, in that culminating miracle—the resurrection of Jesus from the dead—we view again the Trinity in action. Jesus Christ our Lord—to use the Apostle Paul's words in Romans 1:4—"through the Spirit of holiness was declared with power to be the Son of God by his resurrection from the dead."

So, in this mighty, once-for-all act of redemption, the three Persons of the Godhead were participating as one—lovingly, harmoniously, effectively working in behalf of lost humanity. In this personal communication from heaven, God declared His redemptive will for us, even as He had declared His high, moral will earlier at Sinai.

Why would Israel not listen?

There is a question to be considered at this point.

Why did Israel refuse to listen to their God who spoke to them on earth?

First, consider the acceptance of idolatry in Israel's culture and worship. The Israelites had not been able to resist the power of example in Egypt. They had lived among their pagan overlords for 400 years. These heathen masters had dominated their lives. When they saw the Egyptians worshiping their idols, the temptation was there to ask, "Why should we be satisfied with an invisible God? Let us fashion something visible to remind us of Him!"

Then the mighty hand of God—the God who had never forgotten or abandoned His people—delivered these Israelites from slavery and from their pagan surroundings. On the mount, He gave them His Word and His Law. But, as the Bible admits, the children of Israel fell to a new low. They not only committed adultery and fornication in view of the thundering Mount Sinai, but they turned such immoral acts into a religious rite, believing that they could worship Jehovah God with licentious sexual practices.

From the very start of their heathen rituals, the Almighty God condemned them. But although they were His covenant people, they refused to hear and heed the voice of Him who spoke on earth.

There were other areas of disobedience as well. God in His Law had commanded that one day in seven should be observed as a holy and reverent Sabbath. But Israel was largely an agrarian nation, and there were economic reasons for breaking the law of Sabbath rest. If a storm threatened a field of ripe grain, it became easy for the Israelite to finish his harvest on the Sabbath. He would reason within himself, "I know God is not going to be displeased as long as I have a reasonable economic excuse."

We are guilty, too

How do we apply this kind of rationale to our practices in this generation? Surely we must admit that the Israelite farmer of long ago was not alone in his shortcomings! We have become quite adept in our own time in finding and using economic, social and other reasons for doing things we should not do and for making decisions that we should not make. We presume the grace of God is so wide and so flexible that we can do just about anything that pleases us or is convenient, and God will look the other way.

But Jesus was very dogmatic concerning the lives and attitudes of His disciples. We recall how plain and direct His teachings were. Jesus was not concerned at all about the preservation of economic and cultural customs. He said it was most important that His followers should accept the offense of the cross.

I remind you and emphasize it that every serious-minded, committed believer is going to be challenged and even persecuted because he or she is a disciple of the crucified Jesus. Sometimes there are alternatives, both of them good. But at other times, we shall be called upon to take a right and proper stand for Jesus' sake. Jesus did not promise that consistent Christian living would be easy. He did not promise a release from daily problems and pressures. He did not promise to take us home on a fluffy pink cloud.

We live in the knowledge of the grace of God, but we dare not forget that our Lord came to die for us and to express the never-changing moral and redemptive will of God for His people. Before we condemn the Jews of Bible history for their failure, we must be sure we are not overlooking spiritual and moral shortcomings of our own.

The prophetic Scriptures announce a coming day when the restored Jewish remnant will come into a blessed, glorious future. We confess that we are indebted to Israel for many things. We owe them for our Bible, for our Messiah who is now our great High Priest in glory. And when the prophecies of our Lord are fulfilled, restored Israel will again be an effective, God-fearing nation.

But at present, Israel remains under divine judgment. Why? Because Israel rejected the God who loved them, who spoke to them, who cherished them as a chosen people. Israel has turned from the speaking God.

In the light of that history, the writer to the Hebrews has this question for his Christian readers: "If they did not escape when they refused him who warned them on earth, how much less will we, if we turn away from him who warns us from heaven?" (12:25).

We have a personal responsibility

Israel must give her own accounting to God. But what about us? As Christian believers, you and I must be careful about the reasons we give for not heeding God's Word and God's warning from heaven. Have we taken His grace seriously enough that we have asked Him to forgive our spiritual carelessness? Have we identified and dealt with the twin sins of indifference and apathy that are always trying to creep into our daily living?

In our day, we hear strange things concerning the measurement of spiritual life and activity. What measurement will be made of your life if you are among those who insist—sometimes loudly—"I am just as good a Christian as most of the people in our church!"

God's message is clear:

> "Once more I will shake not only the earth but also the heavens." The words "once more" indicate the removing of what can be shaken—that is, created things—so that what cannot be shaken may remain.
>
> Therefore, since we are receiving a kingdom that cannot be shaken, let us be thankful, and so worship God acceptably with reverence and awe, for our "God is a consuming fire." (Hebrews 12:26–29)

The Apostle Peter was in that generation to whom the above words were originally addressed. I close this chapter by telling you that Peter got the message and responded to it! Through Peter, the Holy Spirit has given us one of our best glimpses of the coming shaking of all things and what our preparation should be:

> But the day of the Lord will come like a thief. The heavens will disappear with a roar, the ele-

ments will be destroyed by fire, and the earth and everything in it will be laid bare.

Since everything will be destroyed in this way, what kind of people ought you to be? You ought to live holy and godly lives as you look forward to the day of God and speed its coming. That day will bring about the destruction of the heavens by fire, and the elements will melt in the heat. But in keeping with his promise we are looking forward to a new heaven and a new earth, the home of righteousness. (2 Peter 3:10–13)

Faith Rests on an Unchanging Jesus

MANY ADHERENTS OF CHRISTIANITY are beginning to admit that their attachment is to little more than a pallid "world religion." If they think about it at all, they may wonder where the moral and spiritual dynamic of the early church has gone.

God has humble, faithful people who personally know that moral, spiritual dynamic. "Genuine, effective faith," they will insist, "must always rest on an unchanging Jesus Christ, the same yesterday, today and forever!"

The writer of the Letter to the Hebrews provides us a list of the shining virtues that Christians must exhibit in every generation. And he ties them to the reality of Christ's eternal and divine person:

> Keep on loving each other. . . . Do not forget to entertain strangers. . . . Remember those in prison . . . and those who are mistreated. . . .
>
> Marriage should be honored by all, and the marriage bed kept pure. . . . Keep your lives free from the love of money and be content with what you have. . . .
>
> Remember your leaders, who spoke the word of God to you. Consider the outcome of

their way of life and imitate their faith. Jesus Christ is the same yesterday and today and forever. (Hebrews 13:1–8)

These exhortations are a call to the personal faith and godliness characteristic of the early Christian church. They are based on solid, fundamental Christian doctrine. That is the apostolic method of teaching, instructing and encouraging.

A New Testament pattern

We do not know if Paul was the human writer of this letter, but we can say that this same method of exhortation is apparent in the letters Paul wrote. He first gives his readers the scriptural reasons for certain Christian actions and attitudes. He provides the basis and the reason, and then he exhorts them to respond appropriately.

So it is in this letter. Earlier sections state what Christ has done for the human race and what He now means to the Christian. We are assured that Christ is greater than Moses and Aaron, greater than the angels. We are told that once for all, by His own blood, He purchased mankind's salvation. That is the foundation, and it is strong and true.

Then comes the exhortation: If all of the above is true, then "keep on loving each other." It is a good and gracious argument: because we have reasons for doing something, we ought to do it without delay and without reservations!

Now, in the light of these reasons for exhortation and spiritual action, let me share a thought with you about our modern times and about modern ministries. Quite often we hear a remark that "the

Reverend Doctor John Doe is an inspirational preacher." Frankly, in my judgment there are too many "inspirational" preachers in our day who are trying to cheer up their listeners without using sound, biblical methods.

From my own contacts with them, I describe the "inspirational" preacher like this: after warming his audience with his natural charm, he energetically waves his arms and exhorts people to be a little holier, a little better, a little busier, a little happier and—perhaps—a little more generous. But he fails to give a single compelling reason why they should be any of these things in their daily lives.

It is a method of exhortation without true biblical background or pattern. Suppose you are standing in your own yard, on your lawn, during a quiet summer evening. And suppose I am standing on the sidewalk only a few feet from you. Suddenly I shout at you, "Look out! Jump! Quick!" I reinforce my shout of warning by waving my arms and jumping up and down.

You are not likely to jump. You have no reason to jump—or even to move! You may be puzzled or curious. But you know your yard and your lawn well enough to know there is no compelling reason for you to jump.

But, if I saw you standing on a railroad track and I could also see a speeding train about to run you down and crush out your life, I would surely scream at the top of my lungs, "Jump! Train! Jump quickly!" In that case, there is plenty of reason for action, and you would jump for your life. You might possibly set an unofficial world record for the standing broad jump!

You would be moved to action with good reason. The train is coming, and you will be killed if you do not jump.

I can be very hard to move. If I am being exhorted to action by a man who is merely overheated emotionally, I am likely to drag my feet. I want that man to deal with me on the basis of valid reasons for my interest, my consideration and my decision to act and to move.

Probably you have had some contact with the appeals of ministers who have espoused the cause of liberal Christian theology. Many of them say they want the same piety in people that we want. They want the same honesty, the same loyalty, the same purity, the same degree of philanthropic love expressed for their fellow men. They urge the performance of these good qualities—and quote persuasive poetry along with their urging.

But they fail to provide the good and necessary reasons for these qualities and actions—reasons that are inherent in the Bible and in the proclamation of Christ's saving and keeping gospel.

They want the spiritual virtues without dealing with the root hindrances to such virtues. They want men and women to be more like Jesus, but they want nothing to do with the new birth from above that imprints Jesus' image on people's lives. They want humankind to be forgiving and forgiven, but they do not recognize the biblical necessity for atonement, regeneration and justification. They want the blessing and the display of the fruits of the Spirit, but they reject the Bible's declaration that fruits are related to the fullness of the Spirit.

Actually, they seem to expect fruit and harvest without any tree at all!

We must have a basis for our faith

Their disappointments must be hard for them to explain. The apostolic method was to provide a foundation of good, sound biblical reasons for following the Savior, for our willingness to let the Spirit of God display the great Christian virtues in our lives. That is why we come in faith and rejoicing to the eternal verity of Hebrews 13:8. Because Jesus Christ is eternal and without change forever and ever, we can trust Him and live for Him!

Hebrews 13:8 is the verse of Scripture that gives significance to every other section of teaching and exhortation in the Letter to the Hebrews. In this verse is truth that is moral and spiritual dynamic if we will exercise the faith and the will to demonstrate it in our very needy world.

We hear much discussion about revival and renewal. People talk about spiritual power in the churches. I think this fact—this truth—that Jesus Christ wants to be known in His church as the ever-living, never-changing Lord of all could bring back again the power and the testimony of the early church.

I wonder if you feel like me when I survey much of Christendom in today's world: "They have taken away my Lord and I do not know what they have done with Him!" If we would only seek and welcome our Lord's presence in our midst, we would have the assurance that He is the same Lord He has always been!

As Christian believers, we stand together in the

evangelical faith – the historical faith of our fathers. Yet we must confess that the evangelical church today is bogged down with moral boredom and life-weariness. The church is tired, discouraged and unastonished. Christ seems to belong to yesterday.

The prophetic teachers have projected everything out into the dim future where it is beyond our reach – unavailable. They have dispensationalized us into a state of spiritual poverty – and they have left us there! But regardless of such teachers, the course of spiritual victory is clear: let us trust what the Word of God continues to say to us.

The Scriptures are open and plain

The Scriptures are open and plain. Jesus Christ is our Savior and Lord. He is our great High Priest, alive and ministering for us today. His person, His power and His grace are the same, without change, yesterday, today and forever!

He is the same Lord because He is the same God. He is the same, never having changed in substance, in power, in wisdom, in love, in mercy. In His divine person, Jesus Christ has never known correction or change. He feels now as He has always felt about everyone and everything.

Jesus will not yield to those who charge that He is an absentee, that He is far away and unavailable. Our faith tells us that Jesus Christ is close at hand, that He is a living force in our lives today. He is the Holy Spirit of God fulfilling His promises moment by moment.

We true Christians must stand together in our faith. Our Lord is as powerful now, as real now, as near to us now, as loving now as He ever was when He walked among the men and women on the shores of Galilee. The great spiritual needs around us should drive us back to the gospel records of the life and ministry of our Lord Jesus. When evil men crucified Jesus, killed Him, they had no power to change Him. They could not alter the person and the personality of the Son of God.

Jesus had come for the humiliation of death. He came to declare God's redemptive will. The plotting of jealous men could not destroy His divine affection for a lost race. Putting him on a cross did not drain away any of His love. That is why we believe with assurance and blessing that He is the very same Lord Jesus Christ now!

And it is this ever-living Christ who wants to demonstrate Himself through our faith and love to those around us. How do you suppose Jesus feels today about the sinful men and women who walk our streets? He loves them. No matter how we feel about them, He loves them! We may be righteously indignant about the things they do. We may be disgusted with their actions and ways. We are often ready to condemn them and turn away from them. But Jesus keeps on loving them. It is His unchanging nature to love and to seek the lost.

It is the sick who need a doctor

And how does Jesus feel about the outcasts—the helpless and the hopeless? He said many times when He was on earth, "I have come to help the needy. The well do not need a doctor—but the sick need attention and love!"

By contrast, what is our attitude? We look at the

needy and measure them and say, "Let us determine if they are worthy of our help." I do not think Jesus during all of His ministry on earth ever helped a worthy person. He often asked those who appealed to Him, "What is your need? Do you need My help?"

What would we think of a doctor who would make it known that he would treat or attend only those who could prove themselves well and healthy? What should we think, then, of Christian churches that seem to indicate they have help available only for those who can demonstrate they do not need help?

Jesus is our Lord and Savior. The best thing we know about Him is that He loves the sinner. He has always loved the outcast—and for that we should be glad, for we, too, were once outcasts. We are descended from that first man and woman who failed God and disobeyed. They were cast out of the garden, and God set in place a flaming sword to keep them from returning.

The greatest encouragement throughout the Bible is God's love for His lost race and the willingness of Christ, the eternal Son, to show forth that love in God's plan of redemption. The love of Jesus is so inclusive that it knows no boundaries. At the point where we stop caring and loving, Jesus is still there, loving and caring!

I confess that I like kids. In my congregation, people used to remark that if they could not find me, it was probably because I had run across some little boy or girl delighted to get a piece of candy. But our Lord Jesus loved the children with a kind of love that none of us can even remotely approach.

He loved and gave Himself to the children. It was a special kind of love for all who approached Him in need. And He is still the same today!

Do you ever have times of discouragement? I mean, really rough and depressing periods? Do you have those human times when it is not easy to pray? Do you ever have a week when things are not as fresh and bright as they were the week before? I do, sometimes. And in those times we remember that we are changeable. In our humanness we do change. Thus, we need to remember that Jesus, our Lord, changes not. The manner of our love for one another may change, but the Savior's love remains the same, always constant.

Love one another

This is a good place for me to mention something else about our love for one another within the fellowship of our churches. The writer to the Hebrews appeals to us to "keep on loving each other as brothers" (13:1). In effect he is saying, "You are all born of the same Spirit. You are all witnessing for Christ and waiting for His coming. Therefore, you are to love one another!"

Being the humans that we are, how is it possible for us to love one another in the bonds of our faith? Perhaps this perception of mine will be of help to you.

I have always insisted that it is possible to love people in the Lord even though we may not like them! Here is what I mean. Some people are so nice and friendly and outgoing, so easy to get along with that we have no hesitation about accepting them and loving them. We find it easy to love people like that. But then there are the others! Some are unfriendly. Or perhaps they cut us down. Or just ignore us. Some have personalities that rub us wrong: it may be simply their temperament, or they may be boastful or sarcastic—or ignorant. And we think within ourselves, "It seems impossible for me to like that person!"

I have come to believe that the Bible supports the position that we can *love* such people even if we do not *like* them! We do not like their boorish or distasteful human traits, but we will love them for Jesus' sake.

I am being frank about this, and I hope I am being helpful. Do not ever say that you are not right with God because you like some people more than others. I believe you can be right with God and still not like the way some people behave. Our admonition is to love them in a larger and more comprehensive way because we are all one in Christ Jesus. This kind of love is indeed a Christian virtue, and the Holy Spirit will help us to nurture it and display it in all of our contacts.

It is our responsibility to believe His Word and to obey His truth. It is our task to practice the Christian virtues in the power of the Holy Spirit as we await the coming of Him who will come.

COME LORD JESUS !!